Kingdom Glory Revolutionar Training

The Nehemiah Project- Strategy for Rebuilding

Rebuilding the Walls of Souls, Cities & Nations

Ruth Ann McCormick (RAM)

Copyright@2016RuthAnnMcCormick
All rights reserved, written permission must be secured from the publisher to use or reproduce any part of this book.
Published in Davenport, Fla.
I wish to acknowledge the use of Strong's Hebrew & Greek Dictionary of Words. New American Standard, Amplified, King James, New Revised Standard, New International Versions of the Bible. As well as the American Dictionary & Expository Dictionary.
Ruth Ann McCormick- Kingdom Glory Revolutionaries
Ruth Ann McCormick Contact: Email/kingdombuilderscollege@yahoo.com
Facebook/ Ruth Ann McCormick

The Journey of Rebuilding- Intro

It has been quite a journey of getting to the place of rebuilding and building even anew in my own life. Years of painful processes, healing and dealing. In the beginning, even dealing with numerous generational issues. Traumas and dramas that laid foundations and walls in my life that had to be dismantled because they oppose the Kingdom of God, and prevented me from walking in purpose.

There are times in your life that you may feel like an unwalled city, devastated and wide open to invaders. But I am here to tell you that there is a hope and you have a future. God is concerned about your life, family, Ministry, and has declared success, wholeness, and prosperity over all the above.

God has greater things for you to experience that you may not have presently seen or tapped into yet. 1 Corinthians 2:9 (KJV) "But as it is written, Eye hath not seen, nor ear heard, neither have entered into the heart of man, the things which God hath prepared for them that love him." There is a destined time of restoring and rebuilding appointed for you to undergo in your soul, life, family, Ministry. For these are the first stages of putting together the pieces of a bigger puzzle that God is connecting right before your eyes.

Once you have endured a personal rebuilding and restoring process then the Spirit of God can partner with you in greater dimensions, to bring restoration to Cities and Nations. Because you know what it is like to feel desolate, and looked over due to the destruction and warfare of the enemy. And now you arise from the ashes and the rubble of your past clothed with a mantle of compassion that equips you to assist others who are in need. Isaiah 61:4 (AMP) "And they shall rebuild the ancient ruins; they shall raise up the former desolations and renew the ruined cities, the devastations of many generations."

I pray that you are able to glean something of substance from this teaching. That even through these pages the Spirit of God will release to you a blueprint, a strategy for your own rebuilding project.

Ruth Ann McCormick
Kingdom Glory Revolutionaries

Getting Started

This booklet is to inform you of a Vision and a Strategy. The moment we receive Jesus in our hearts we become God's Sons and Daughters. There is an assignment on our lives that we were given to fulfill. As well as a mandate that was given to all in Genesis 1:26 26 Then God said, "Let us make mankind in our image, in our likeness, so that they may rule over the fish in the sea and the birds in the sky, over the livestock and all the wild animals, and over all the creatures that move along the ground."

We are to be busy readying the Nations of this World for the return of our King. We do this by taking dominion and authority; ruling and reigning in Christ Jesus. Being the instruments, the vessels that God uses to plow and till, rebuild and restore the land. Time to yield the swords of war in the highways and the byways offending the enemy and defending what is the God of heaven and earth's people and possessions.

Sons and Daughters are crying out, "Prepare ye the way for the Lord." Going forth as His hands and feet in the land, being extended forth to a lost and dying world. Are you compelled to GO YE and compel those to come in? It is time that we emerge from the 4 walls and fulfill our mandate and call.

If you are interested and desire to be a part of this program, a strategy from heaven, we welcome you and look forward to co-laboring with you in any way possible to see His Kingdom that has already Come, be established. To see lives changed, souls won, territories transformed and a culture shift in society. To take back the land that the enemy has stolen. And become faithful and dedicated to the Genesis Mandate, taking our dominion in the earth.

Chapters

1. Story of Nehemiah- Strategy……………………8

2. The Gates of Hell Shall Not Prevail…………18

3. Who I Am……………………………………………24

4. Soul Fragmentation & Invasion………………26

5. Rebuilding the Walls of Your Life…………32

6. Nehemiah Project……………………………………38

7. Nehemiah Burden & Prayer……………………44

8. Unfolding of the Plan……………………………47

9. Implementation of the Plan……………………49

10. Let Us Arise & Build……………………………54

11. Believe God Will Grant You Success…………58

12. The Gates Need to be Restored………………67

13. Completion………………………………… 76

14. Strategy from Nehemiah…………… 79

15. Working of the Nehemiah Strategy…… 81

16. Scriptures to Assist the Rebuilding Rebuilding….83

1.
Story of Nehemiah – A Strategy

First It Is Personal

The Book of Nehemiah is filled with strategy; a blueprint from heaven that was divinely inspired and documented for us to establish heaven on earth. This story is illustrative of the brokenness of the soul of man as well as of Territories and Nations. And how the Sovereignty of God, the great mercies of God brought forth all that was needed to ensure a rebuilding process.

God's Word promises us that restoration is our portion, Joel 2:25 (KJV) "I will restore to you the years that the locust hath eaten, the cankerworm, and the caterpillar, and the palmerworm, my great army which I sent among you." God knew that mankind, His creation was going to endure situations that would position us in the place of needing restoration. Being the loving, merciful God that He is, once again provision was made for our brokenness.

We always refer to worms and locust as those destructive forces that come to devour and destroy our crops, our fields of harvest. And yet in the midst is the caterpillar- the very thing that is symbolic for a transformation process that takes place, even in our own lives after accepting Christ. The caterpillar is a scavenger, it feeds and sustains itself on whatever growth it can find. So many times, we as a caterpillar, in our immaturity will even cause ourselves destruction.

I have thought about the fact that a caterpillar is a scavenger and it eats whatever foliage and greenery it can find to sustain itself. This is like a new convert, or a Christian that is in the midst of their transformation process. So many times they will eat whatever they can find because they are hungry. Even with no regard to whether or not it is a good source of nutrition or not. The caterpillar does not care as long as it fills its stomach and curbs that yearning in its depths to be fed. This comes with a danger, because if they eat contaminated or poisonous food it could stunt their growth or cause death.

A hungry caterpillar does not think about the source of food that they are feeding on, that once chewed up will be a part of who they are. The fact that it might be a weed or a poisonous plant that will make them sick afterwards, is not an issue when it is satisfying that void in their depths. Because they are hungry, and have an emptiness longing to be filled. They have a desire- a zealous need to eat food, and to experience life and grow. I can clearly relate this to myself as a new convert and even the years following as I was maturing in Christ.

I was like a caterpillar, running from vine to vine, branch to branch, place to place to be fed. Sometimes the food that I found to feed on because I was operating out of zeal and lacked wisdom at that point, was not always beneficial to me. We are admonished to use wisdom, 1 John 4:1 (AMP) "Beloved, Do not put faith In every spirit, but prove (test) the spirits to discover whether they proceed from God; for many false prophets have gone forth into the world."

The food I ate that was bad for me did in fact become a part of who I was. So now, because I ate bad food, and did not discern that it was bad food; due to the fact that I was running around grazing from every pasture out of zeal- I was in need of healing and in some cases more deliverance, not to mention some deprogramming. Thus making my transformation process even a more painful journey. Revelation 2:20 (AMP) "But I have this against you: that you tolerate the woman Jezebel, who calls herself a prophetess (claiming to be inspired), and who is teaching and leading astray my servants and beguiling them into practicing sexual vice and eating food sacrificed to idols."

Clearly that scripture says to us that we are held accountable for what we allow to enter into our gates, our soul. God addressed the Church in Thyatira, Genesis 2:19 (NIV) "I know your deeds, your love and faith, your service and perseverance, and that you are now doing more than you did at first." God saw all the good things that they were accomplishing but he was not happy with them even in the sight of all they did. The reason being was because they were partakers of the teachings that defiled and mislead them. Allowing error into our gates, our souls, is like eating the teachings of Jezebel.

I believe we all have endured those times that we have been our own worst enemy, devouring our own crops. Even at times being used to hinder and or devour the crops and or growth of others. The enemy manipulating us to bring confusion or destruction instead of restoration. These are signs of one that needs to undergo their own transformation process and become what their DNA has already predestined them to become. A beautiful butterfly, created by the hand of God, soaring on the winds of the Spirit of God.

Once we undergo our own transformation process we will no longer be as the caterpillar devouring and being destructive. But we will be known and seen as one that is reflecting the light and Glory of God. 2 Corinthians 5:17 (KJV) "Therefore if any man be in Christ, he is a new creature: old things are passed away; behold, all things are become new."

Many have endured much hardness either by their own mistakes and lack of wisdom; or at the hands of others being used by the enemy of their soul. Hosea 4:6 (KJV) "My people perish from a lack of knowledge". Knowledge and wisdom come from experiences as well as learned; it is a byproduct of maturity and growth.

If you are in a caterpillar stage, you are still at the suffering and obtaining knowledge part of your transformation process. 2 Corinthians 1:7 (KJV) "And our hope of you is steadfast, knowing, that as ye are partakers of the sufferings, so shall ye be also of the consolation." 1 Peter 4:13 (NIV) "But rejoice inasmuch as you participate in the sufferings of Christ, so that you may be overjoyed when his glory is revealed."

In this season of your life you will make mistakes and even have some regrets from decisions you made that proved to be the wrong ones. Also due to lack of wisdom and other influences you may come to regret things that you have done or said. The enemy strategizes to use these vulnerabilities, character flaws and issues against us as we are transforming to reflect the image and nature of Christ. The desire of the enemy is to stop progression in the process. Your enemies' goal is to steal, kill and destroy; so it conspires against you in hopes that you will die in the process.

For if we do not go forward and allow ourselves to transform, conform and become what and who the DNA that God has placed within us dictates, we will die in the process. Because we refuse to become who we were created to become, our DNA within us is a life force that is constantly working from our depths to get us to reflect the intended purpose for our being.

Look at the butterfly, which is such a wonderful example. He begins as a caterpillar and embarks on a life changing transformation process. Once he crawled around on the ground, all he knew was valleys and low places. Then once transformation is completed, he soars in the high places. But he first had to endure the darkness and isolation of the cocoon.

The cocoon is prophetic for that night season, alone season, that nothing makes any sense season. It is here in the midst of isolation and uncertainty that the caterpillar is being transformed by an inward working of his DNA. The caterpillar only had to surrender to the cocoon and his DNA. Then after his surrender, the creative power deposited within him begins to transform and conform him into the image that God created and destined him to reflect.

If the caterpillar refuses to undergo the season of the cocoon, he is refusing to surrender to his DNA and his created purpose. This rebellion unto his DNA will cause him to die in the process. He cannot remain as a caterpillar, which was his identity for only a season and time. Many have refused to undergo their transformation process, enduring the cocoon. And they suffer the consequences of dying within themselves in the midst of a process that was to be a birthing process into a new identity as well as a new way of life. 2 Corinthians 5:17-19 (NIV) "Therefore, if anyone is in Christ, he is a new creation; the old has gone, the new has come! All this is from God, who reconciled us to himself in Christ, and gave us the ministry of reconciliation: that God was reconciling the world to himself in Christ, not counting men's sins against them. And he was committed to the message of reconciliation."

God was and is committed to reconciling us to Him, we should be just as committed in allowing ourselves to be reconciled to Him. Likewise, we should be committed to reflecting the image of one that has been reconciled unto God. Our flesh, our will, can be stubborn, and resist the process by not surrendering our soul to the process.

This process ordained by God and accomplished by the hand of God, just requires your cooperation. Ephesians 4:22-24 (NAS) "that, in reference to your former manner or life, you lay aside the old self, which is being corrupted in accordance with the lusts of deceit. And that you be renewed in the spirit of your mind, and put on the new self, which in the likeness of God has been created in righteousness and holiness of truth." Isaiah 42:9 (NAS) "Behold, the former things have come to pass, Now I declare new things; before they spring forth I proclaim then to you."

Rebellion to the will of God for our life causes us to die in the midst of a process. One that should cause us to birth forth into abundant life that was promised. I am reemphasizing this point on purpose, it is important we understand the importance of our surrendering to the process. Psalms 16:11 (KJV) "Thou wilt show me the path of life: in thy presence is fullness of joy; at thy right hand there are pleasures for evermore." John 10:10 (KJV) "The thief cometh not, but for to steal, and to kill, and to destroy: I am come that they might have life, and that they might have it more abundantly."
Isaiah 43:19-21 (NAS) "Behold, I will do something new, now it will spring forth; will you not be aware of it? I will even make a roadway in the wilderness, rivers in the desert. The beasts of the field will glorify Me, the jackals and the ostriches. Because I have given waters in the wilderness, and rivers in the desert. To give drink to My chosen people. The people whom I formed for Myself will declare My praise."

Walls of Salvation

As individuals, we have faced adversities and levels of trauma throughout our lives that at times have left us feeling broken down as a City without walls. Our souls have known the pillaging of the enemy as we were overtaken at times and raided. The enemy took advantage of our condition and invaded us as our defenses were down and we were vulnerable. The invasions of the enemy that tormented and wounded us to the point that we even placed walls of protection around our souls, which were built on the bricks and mortar of bitterness, pain, and unforgiveness.

Building these protective walls of self-defense, we did so believing that we were girded and protected from any further pain or betrayal. Only to find that our walls kept our healer Jehovah-Raphe out, and boxed the pain in, within our borders; tormenting us and gnawing at us from the inside out. Terrorism of another form, the enemy invaded our borders, raided our life and left a trail of devastation. Walls erected to keep out any intruders or further wounding and now we are alone, isolated, and bleeding from the inside out.

The enemy of our soul was able to break through our defenses and bombard the walls, hedge of protection that God places around us. Maybe it was our choices, lack of discipline or disobedience; or maybe it was a learning experience that we must endure to gain knowledge and wisdom. Proverbs 25:28 (KJV) "He that hath no rule over his own spirit is like a city that is broken down, and without walls". Proverbs 25:28 (NLT)" A person without self-control is like a city with broken-down walls."

We choose whom we shall serve, every day of our lives. Will we be self-controlled, disciplined and walk in the Spirit and not be led by our flesh and emotions? Whether we are aware or not, our actions determine who we are really serving on a daily basis; flesh, the enemy of our soul, or the lover of our soul. Who we decide to serve will reflect in our lives in many ways.

Lacking self –control and discipline will cause us to be as an unwalled city; the enemy will be able to easily invade and trespass, for our defenses are broken down. In our midst will be a trail of devastation and pain; a broken life because of broken down walls of protection. Then we find that we are in a place of despair and in need of repair.

The enemy strategizes to invade a City, Nation, and our territory in regards to geographical location or even the boundaries of your soul. But before the actual strike there is spying of the land- the enemy does some recon; to check defenses and see if the borders are penetrable. Then, if possible he will erect his own walls of demonically enforced lies. These are strategically placed, to build his fortress from which he can rule and reign over your soul, or a territory. The lies, issues that are contrary to the Word of God, which are strategically released and if not overthrown by us, His carriers of light and truth; become the foundations and walls of the enemy's stronghold in our midst.

It is from these strongholds that the enemy of our soul is now empowered and begins to lead and govern over lives and territories from. All began with the lies that he imbeds in the depths of a soul that one begins to believe as truth. This is why we need to guard our souls and ensure that it is as a fortified City, protected against the wiles of the enemy. We are admonished to allow the mind of Christ to prosper in us, Romans 12:2 (NAS) "And do not be conformed to this world, but be transformed by the renewing of your mind, so that you may prove what the will of God is, that which is good and acceptable and perfect." Spirit of God spoke to me once that in order to be a watchmen over territories and regions and govern nations; we must first be a watchmen over our own soul and govern our own territory first.

The Stronghold

Picture if you will a Principality over a city, see its stronghold from which it is ruling and reigning from. To help with the visual, see a castle, a fortress like in medieval times. Now picture gatekeepers that protect the gates and entrances, and the guards that secure the fortress and protect it. The Principality is as a king over this kingdom, and he has messengers that deliver lies to unsuspecting victims. Along the walls of this fortress there are as well archers that shoot fiery arrows, darts of destruction at anyone who is a threat or opposition to their king or the stronghold that they protect.

With each lie that the victim believes as truth, now there is a connection between that person and a demonic power attempting to rule and reign over them. Not only that, but the lie as well acts as an open door for a demonic stronghold over a city to begin to adversely influence you. Under these circumstances you are not just contending with the power of a stronghold in your mind, but that which is of even greater demonic influence that is empowering it. This enemy has invaded your atmosphere, as well as the territory that you dwell in.

If you have a demonic stronghold in your mind or your emotions it is like an invisible umbilical cord in the spirit that yokes you, connects you spiritually in the unseen realm with a power of darkness over a City. This attachment-lie if not broken, by renewing the mind with Gods' truth will continue to be an access into the life it has attached to0, and who the lie is now embedded in. Now the demonic power is able to feed the person more lies easily, it already has access.

That is why we cannot afford to be as an unwalled city, undisciplined. Nor can we afford to lack in accountability for the condition of our own souls. We must renew our mind and allow the mind of Christ that we have been given to prosper. 1 Corinthians 2:16 (NIV) "For who has known the mind of the Lord that he may instruct him? But we have the mind of Christ." This shuts down the access to our lives, which spirits and forces of darkness if possible can have.

We cannot afford to be lacking in sensitivity to God and know His mind and will this hour. Our focus must be on God, His Kingdom and His truth so we are not affected or influenced by the atmosphere that maybe prevailing in our city or region. If possible the very elect will be deceived, Mark 8:33 (NIV) "But when Jesus turned and looked at His disciples, he rebuked Peter. "Get behind me, Satan!" he said. "You do not have in mind the things of God, but the things of men."

It Begins With Self

The first stages of a broad scale rebuilding or restoring process is to experience this move in your own life as an individual. Beginning with the mind, because this will position you in a better place in the spirit. Once we have been transformed and renewed in our minds, and have pulled down strongholds and dealt with old mindsets. Then we can access life of the Spirit in a new measure. Romans 8:5-8 (NAS) "For those who are according to the flesh set their minds on the things of the flesh, but those who are according to the Spirit, the things of the Spirit. For the mind set on the flesh is death, but the mind set on the Spirit is life and peace, because the mind set on the flesh is hostile toward God; for it does not subject itself to the law of God, for it is not even able to do so."

Think about that scripture a moment, the mind of the flesh is hostile towards God. Hostile is being in opposition to, an enemy of. Clearly we can see the condition of our mind does so influence our right standing with God. We are held accountable for the condition of our own souls. Have we become undisciplined, are we standing in the midst of rubble all around us- the rubble of our life, an unwalled city?

In some cases we have been a victim and our walls of protection are laying like a pile of rubble around our lives. 2 Chronicles 36:19 (NIV) "They set fire to God's temple and broke down the wall of Jerusalem; they burned all the palaces and destroyed everything of value there." The next step we take is to enter into a process of healing and deliverance. This takes place in our soul as we pull down demonically built walls that enforce strongholds, the lies of the enemy. These lies of the enemy and subsequent strongholds of the enemy oppose the Spirit of God from touching us in our depths. Not to mention they as well restrict the power of God that is to be released from our depths.

It is pertinent that during these times of healing and restoration that we speak God's Word over our lives and situation. Ezra 9:9 (NIV) "Though we are slaves, our God has not deserted us in our bondage. He has shown us kindness in the sight of the kings of Persia: He has granted us new life to rebuild the house of our God and repair its ruins, and he has given us a wall of protection in Judah and Jerusalem." Nehemiah 2:17 (NIV) "Then I said to them, "You see the trouble we are in: Jerusalem lies in ruins, and its gates have been burned with fire. Come, let us rebuild the wall of Jerusalem, and we will no longer be in disgrace." Zechariah 2 (NIV) "3 Then the angel who was speaking to me left, and another angel came to meet him 4 and said to him: "Run, tell that young man, 'Jerusalem will be a city without walls because of the great number of men and livestock in it. 5 And I myself will be a wall of fire around it,' declares the LORD, 'and I will be its glory within." Zechariah 2:5 "And I myself will be a wall of fire around it,' declares the Lord,' and I will be its glory within."

Even Job, one of the most faithful and blessed men there were was found himself tested and tried by the enemy. Job 1:10 (NIV) "Have you not put a hedge around him and his household and everything he has? You have blessed the work of his hands, so that his flocks and herds are spread throughout the land. Job 1:12 "All right, you may test him," the LORD said to Satan. "Do whatever you want with everything he possesses, but don't harm him physically." So Satan left the LORD's presence.

Let God know you want His walls around your life, also that after your own restoration you want to be used to restore and stand in the gap for others walls that need to be rebuilt in others' lives, cities and Nations. Ezekiel 22:30 "I searched for a man among them who would build up the wall and stand in the gap before Me, for the land, so that I would not destroy it; but I found no one." Isaiah 58:12 "Those from among you will rebuild the ancient ruins; you will raise up the age-old foundations; and you will be called the repairer of the breach, the restorer of the streets in which to dwell."

Personal Inventory- What Is Making Up Your Walls That Need To Be Dismantled? Or What Is In The Rubble That Needs To Be Rebuilt?

1.

2.

3.

4.

5.

6.

7.

8.

9.

10.

2.
The Gates of Hell Shall Not Prevail

Declarations to Develop the Mind of Christ

Father, I come to you through your Son- Jesus, boldly approaching the throne of Grace to obtain mercy. I am declaring and decreeing over myself that the same mind that is in Christ Jesus is in me. This same mind that is in Christ Jesus is prospering in my midst and causing an inward revolution from the revelation that I am receiving from the mind of God. For your thoughts are Truth and because of that as I tap into your thoughts, I can know the truth and by the truth be set free.

Father, I declare in the Name of Jesus that every stronghold, mindset, thought and imagination that prevents me from giving and receiving unconditional love is pulled down in Jesus Name. 1 Corinthians 13 says: "If I speak in the tongues of men or of angels, but do not have love, I am only a resounding gong or a clanging cymbal. " I declare I am not and will not just be a clanging cymbal making noise without purpose or power, for I am a vessel of love, and I release this love that covers a multitude of sins to all. I declare I will not keep a record of suffered wrongs. Nor will I be fearful, for perfect love casts out all fear. The assignment of fear is canceled and every fear of being rejected, dejected, used and abused again, leaves from my mind-NOW – in Jesus Name.

I declare my thoughts line up to your Word; Phil.2:3 "Let nothing be done through strife or vainglory; but in lowliness of mind let each esteem the other better than themselves."

I declare that the Mind of Christ is equipping and enabling me by the Spirit of God to comply with James 4:7 "Submit yourselves therefore to God. Resist the devil, and he will flee from you."

I declare that the mind of Christ which is in agreement with the Spirit of God is enabling me to be obedient unto God. Not in my own strength but in God's might and power, his ability given to me to fulfill and comply with the Word of God.

I declare not by might nor by power but it is by His Spirit that I'm able to fulfill, comply and be obedient to His Word which produces life.

I declare Ephesians 4:22-29 over myself.

"That ye put off concerning the former conversation the old man, which is corrupt according to deceitful lusts. And be renewed in the spirit of your mind. And that ye put on the new man, which after God is created in righteousness and true holiness. Wherefore putting away lying, speak every man truth with his neighbor, for we are members one of another. Be ye angry, and sin not; let not the sun go down upon your wrath: Neither give place to the devil. Let no corrupt communication proceed out of your mouth, but that which is good to the use of edifying, that it may minister grace to the hearers."

I declare that I am no longer tormented or harassed in my mind or emotions by past offenses, nor do the words that once slandered and wounded me echo in my mind any longer. The mind of Christ is driving out all the past torments and memories that aligned with and fed my emotions to keep me in a place of bondage. I choose to forgive so I am released from these torments and tormentors in Jesus Name! I forgive so I can be forgiven. I can be assured that I am free for your Word declares, "He that the Son has set free is free indeed!" I come forth-NOW- out of every prison cell of the past, every incarceration in my mind, and I walk in the freedom, which Christ Jesus has given me. For I have been given the mind of Christ.

I declare that I do not have an identity crisis. I know who I am in Christ. In 2 Corinthians 5:21 your Word says, "I am the righteousness of God." In Ephesians 2:10 you said I am your workmanship created in Christ Jesus for good works.

I declare that I have the power and authority to do as your word tells me to do in reference to strongholds in my mind. I do pull down every thought and imagination and take captive that which would exalt itself against the knowledge of Christ Jesus.

I declare that I am in agreement with what the Word of God says concerning me and who I am in Christ. I reject the enemy's thoughts and opinions concerning me. I speak to every stronghold of rejection and pull it down, and I speak to every confusion that would attempt to enter into my thought life and I declare your assignment is canceled and your power is stripped in Jesus Name.

I declare that all forms of rejection that breed confusion into one's identity and that causes one to be double minded; your every stronghold and mindset are dismantled now in Jesus Name! I declare I am free to find, know, and walk in my identity- call, purpose, and destiny of God. For the thoughts that my Abba Father has concerning me are becoming my thoughts. For your thoughts God are higher than mine and your ways are likewise higher than mine. I declare your higher thoughts are making a highway for me this day out of the wilderness called identity crisis-in Jesus Name!

I declare that the Spirit of Sonship, spirit of adoption, penetrates my mind, and that I will continually call out Abba Father. With the knowledge that I am a son and no longer a child or a slave. I declare I possess the knowledge that I am a Son and no longer a child. I am a son of God that is predestined and blessed by a father that knows how to give good gifts. One such gift is the knowledge that I have been given that enforces my identity as a son of God. This is an unshakeable truth in my depths- "I AM ACCEPTED IN HE BELOVED." This is a personal revelation as well as my reality.

I declare that the mind of Christ, the mind of the Spirit has freed me from the law of sin and death. For the carnal mind and thoughts are what kept me attached to death that opposes the abundant life I have been promised. I am free from the carnal mind, and its death thoughts. Now I shall experience the John 10:10 life more abundant that has been promised to me, in Jesus Name!

I declare the victorious mind of Christ emerges and takes over my thought life displacing all thoughts of defeat, hopelessness, abuse and victimization. I declare the victim mentality that kept me yoked to poverty is broken off my mind and my life. I declare the yoke of poverty is removed from my soul as well as every area of my life, family, and Ministry unto the Lord in Jesus Name.

I declare insecurity has no place in my thoughts or in my life in Jesus Name.

I declare 3 John 1:2, that as I am allowing this inward transformation to take place in my soul, my mind, will, intellect and emotions- I shall know, see and experience the prosperity of the Kingdom of God in every area of my life that God has declared shall prosper.

I declare that I am standing at the banks of my Red Sea experience. And I do trust my God to deliver me. Just as you God spoke to the Israelites, I believe it is as well for me. "After this day the enemies I see I shall see no more." For the blood of Jesus has set me free from all my past captors and tormentors that attempted to keep me in Egypt. I as well declare that my thought life will not resurrect a tormentor, or a captivating thought, out from under the blood of Jesus. I will not dig it up, revisit it, think on it or meditate on any past wounds or situations that enslaved me. My mind will not resurface the offenses and the offenders of my past in Jesus Name. For I have been given all power and authority through Christ Jesus and I take this authority and I pull down the Egypt mentality and I declare the mind of Christ that leads me out and to my Promised Land!

I declare that I am blessed, blessed coming in and blessed going out. Blessed in the field and the basket. I am so blessed men are giving unto my bosom. For the blessings of God are overtaking every situation that does not yet line up to the blessings and goodness of God. I declare that he who hanged on the tree became the curse for me, so I cannot be- I am not- cursed. I pull down every thought, imagination, and all mindsets that support and give curses access to my life through the law. I tear down every religious structure in my mind, and evict every religious thought. I declare the blood of Jesus is washing away even the residue of these thoughts and or teachings that I absorbed that were of error concerning this. I am blessed and cannot be cursed, for what God has blessed cannot be cursed. I will not live like, talk like, act like I am cursed. For I am not cursed for the Shout of the King is among me. And where sin abounds, grace abounds much more.

I declare that everything that has been erected in my mind by doctrines of man-teachings of Jezebel; and of error, or trauma and drama experienced in my life that has attempted to block my destiny is driven out of my mind and my life in Jesus Name. For just as you spoke over Joshua, every piece of ground that my feet step on is mine to possess. The Spirit of God is currently going before me and driving out every spiritual "ITE" that stands between me and my Promised Land. I declare my mind is saturated with Truth and I am a possessor of the promises of God, in Jesus Name!

I declare that even my thoughts about myself are lining up to God's thoughts towards me. For whatsoever a man thinketh in his heart so is he?

I declare that every thought and imagination associated with sickness, disease and infirmity- you are cast down in Jesus name. I do not believe the report of or the lies of the enemy, nor will I align with any lying symptoms that currently maybe making themselves known in my physical being. I declare 1 Peter 2:24, by the stripes of Jesus I am healed. I believe my body is manifesting this Truth. I am every wit whole, healed, manifesting God's healing words of truth in Jesus Name. For I believe the truth of God's word and not the report and lies of the enemy. I am healed and whole from the inside out; spirit, soul (mind & emotions) and body. No weapon formed against me shall prosper in Jesus name!

I declare I operate from the mind of Christ, in Jesus Name!

I declare wisdom, understanding, revelation of God is prospering my soul, in Jesus Name.

I declare all the old religious strongholds, beliefs, thought patterns, are being replaced by truth and victorious- Kingdom of God thought patterns, in Jesus Name!

I declare that I am humble, even in the attitude of my mind. That I know who I am in Christ but, I as well remain submissive and obedient to the King of Kings and Lord of Lord's who is my Creator and Lover of my soul. For I am instructed in Proverbs 3: 7, "Be not wise in thy own eyes, fear the Lord and turn from evil."

I declare Romans 12:2 over my life, "Do not conform any longer to the pattern of this world, but be transformed by the renewing of your mind. Then you will be able to test and approve what God's will is- his good, pleasing and perfect will." I will not conform but be ye transformed, and I will renew my mind by meditating on the Word of God, and being in the presence of God. Grace of God conforming me to reflect the image of God.

I declare the mind of Christ is causing my mind to become stable, no longer am I double minded or unstable and wavering. For as the Word of God says, if such was the case I am not to expect to receive anything from God. Hebrews 10:23 says, let us hold fast to the profession of our faith without wavering. The mind of Christ is bringing me to a place of not wavering between two opinions, but being single minded in thought- the mind of Christ prevailing.

I declare the spirit of counsel can operate through me, for I have the mind of Christ. 1 Corinthians 2:16, "For who hath known the mind of the Lord, that he may instruct him? But we have the mind of Christ.

I declare and apply Philippians 4:8 to my life and I guard my thought life with all diligence. "Finally, brethren, whatsoever things are true, whatsoever things are honest, whatsoever things are just, whatsoever things are pure, whatsoever things are lovely, whatsoever things are of good report; if there be any virtue, and if there be any praise, think on these things."

I declare that with the mind of Christ operating in me, I can be sober, alert and vigilant. As well as possess the higher thoughts of God that conform me inwardly and provoke my actions to become those that support holiness. 1 Peter 1:13-16, "Therefore, with minds that are alert and fully sober, set your hope on the grace to be brought to you when Jesus Christ is revealed at his coming. As obedient children, do not conform to the evil desires you had when you lived in ignorance. But just as he who called you is holy, so be holy in all you do; for it is written: Be holy, because I am holy."

I declare that I am not darkened in the understanding of my mind, I am putting off the old self and being made new in the attitude of my mind. Ephesians 4:17-24 " So I tell you this, and insist on it in the Lord, that you must no longer live as the Gentiles do, in the futility of their thinking. They are darkened in their understanding and separated from the life of God because of the ignorance that is in them due to the hardening of their hearts. Having lost all sensitivity, they have given themselves over to sensuality so as to indulge in every kind of impurity, and they are full of greed. That, however, is not the way of life you learned when you heard about Christ and were taught in him in accordance with the truth that is in Jesus. You were taught, with regard to your former way of life, to put off your old self, which is being corrupted by its deceitful desires, to be made new in the attitude of your minds; and to put on the new self, created to be like God in true righteousness and holiness."

3.
Who I Am In Christ

I am A Child of God (Romans 8:16)
I am redeemed from the hand of the enemy (Psalms 107:2)
I am one delivered from the power of darkness (Colossians 1:13, 14)
I am saved by Grace through Faith (Ephesians 2:8)
I am justified (Romans 5:11)
I am sanctified (I Corinthians 6:11)
I am a new creature (2 Corinthians 5:17)
I am a partaker of His Divine Nature (2Peter 1:4)
I am redeemed from the curse of the law (Galatians 3:13)
I am led by the Spirit of God (Romans 8:14)
I am a son of God (Romans 8:14)
I am kept in safety wherever I go (Psalms 91:11)
I am getting all my needs met by Jesus (1 Peter 5:7)
I am strong in the Lord and in the Power of His Might (Ephesians 6:10)
I am casting all my cares on Jesus (1Peter 5:7)
I am doing all things through Christ who strengthens me (Philippians 4:13)
I am an heir of God and a joint heir with Jesus (Romans 8:17)
I am heir to the blessing of Abraham (Galatians 3: 13, 14)
I am blessed coming in and blessed going out (Deuteronomy 28:6)
I am an heir of eternal life (1John 5:11, 12)
I am blessed with all spiritual blessings (Ephesians 1:3)
I am healed by His stripes (1 Peter 2:24)
I am exercising my authority over the enemy (Luke 10:19)
I am more than a conqueror (Romans 8:37)
I am an overcomer by the blood of the Lamb and the Word of My Testimony (Rev 12:11)
I am daily overcoming the devil (1John 4:4)
I am not moved by what I see (2Corinthians 4:18)
I am walking by faith and not by sight (2 Corinthians 5:7)
I am casting down vain imaginations (2 Corinthians 10:4-5)
I am bringing every thought into captivity (2 Corinthians 10:5)
I am being transformed by the renewing of my mind (Romans 12:1, 2)
I am a laborer together with God (1 Corinthians 3:9)
I am the righteousness of God in Christ (2 Corinthians 5:21)
I am a follower of Jesus (Ephesians 5:1)
I am the light of the world (Matthew 5:14)

I am blessing the Lord at all times and continually praising the Lord with my mouth (Psalms 34:1)

4.
Soul Fragmentation Opens You Up For Invasion

Broken Walls, Broken Heart

Nelsons' Expository Dictionary of the Old Testament defines restoration as, "To heal may be described as restoring to normal, an act which God typically performs." In other words, even physical healing, or any healing for that matter, can be classified as a form of restoration. This is an act of restoring back to a state that one should have originally been.

We are currently focusing on dealing with the walls of your soul as an individual, being whole in your depths. Issues of life, wounding, betrayals, trauma and drama can cause soul fragmentation. To describe soul fragmentation in a way that is literal. Picture a glass vase, now take that vase and throw it on a hard tile or concrete floor. That glass is now a shattered mess, slivers, pieces of fragmented glass scattered everywhere. Sadly this is the condition and state of some that are even reading this right now.

I pray right now that the Spirit of God would move in your midst and touch every broken, wounded, fragmented place within your soul. That God would do what only He can do in your depths to make you whole again. That the brokenness of your soul will be the beginning of a new work in your life.

Soul fragmentation is a splitting or an advanced form of compartmentalizing of your soul. The main aim behind soul fragmentation is the removal of your conscience and the breaking of your will, stripping your connection with God. Making you more vulnerable to the enemy. Fragmenting creates vacancies, empty slots within your soul for spirits to take up residence or oppress.

Think of a hotel and all its rooms that are available for occupants. If a soul has been damaged and bruised, fragmented so that it is not whole, then it is compartmentalized. Like the hotel with all its defined room spaces available for occupancy. With so many possible visitors, one that has been fragmented in their soul will deal with at times a lot of confusion and double mindedness.

Salvation opens the lines of communication between the spirit and the soul. Deliverance cuts the lines of communication between the demonic realm and the soul. But even still, after salvation and deliverance the soul needs healing/restoration.

Since the fall of man at the Garden, our souls have been enduring fragmentations, abuses, and wounding. Psalms 41:4 "I said, Lord, be merciful to me; heal my soul; for I have sinned against thee." We need to experience Psalms 23:3, "He restoreth my soul; he leadeth me in the paths of righteousness for His names' sake."

Root Causes of Fragmentation

Any and all sin will tear and fracture a soul. Some sins tear the soul more than others. Sexual soul ties can be very damaging. Proverbs 6:32 "But whosoever committeth adultery with a woman lacketh understanding he that doeth it destroyeth his own soul." When two people become one and then separate, the tie that was formed between the two souls is torn, tearing the souls in the process. This is why divorces, and breakups at times feel like a death. In your depths there is a severing of the soul tie and it is in a death process.

When the process is repeated over and over, the soul becomes very much damaged. I Corinthians 6:16 "Or do you not know that he who is joined to a harlot is one body with her? For the two, he says shall become one flesh." Literally with every sexual partner a person has, they become more fragmented. I will break this down a little bit more. Suzy slept with Johnny and she may have been a virgin, but Johnny has been with 10 other girls. Johnny had intercourse with 10 partners and became as one flesh with them. There was a soul tie made with each of these ten girls, between Johnny and them. Suzy has now by sleeping with Johnny entered into a demonic multiplication factoring.

Johnny slept with ten other than Suzy, so Suzy slept with 11+ people. She slept with Johnny and made a soul tie with him, who had soul ties with the previous ten girls. Not only that, but in addition to that, whoever the girls had slept with and developed a soul tie with. This much fragmentation and brokenness makes one real vulnerable for a transference of spirits through these soul ties.

I knew a young lady who had sexual relations with a man that was bipolar. Shortly afterwards this same young lady began to manifest symptoms of being bipolar. She had no symptoms of such prior, nor was it an issue in her bloodline. Not only did she need deliverance and healing as a result of the soul tie but now she had other issues to contend with.

Witchcraft, drugs, false religions, abuses, alcohol, idolatry can all erode and fragment a soul. There are many causes that lead up to soul fragmentation, but the end result is the same- a soul in need. A person who is dealing with a fragmented soul will display emotional highs and lows, double minded, emotionally and or mentally unstable.

A fragmented soul greatly impacts ones' ability to think, discern, and judge soberly. Fragmentation impairs a soul to the point a lot of times that the person will experience confusion. Deep inward pain drives them at times to develop habits or ways of coping and escaping. Addictive patterns and behaviors can be a result of a soul that is fragmented and the pain becomes greater than their ability to deal with it.

Soul fragmentation can happen if we are not properly aligned within ourselves as well. If the soul is "KING", we are sure to engage in some form of sin against God. The door has been opened and the enemy of your soul will take advantage of the opportunity given to him. Psalms 7: 1-2 "God! God! I am running to you for dear life; the chase is wild. If they catch me, I'm finished; ripped to shreds by foes fierce as lions, dragged into the forest and left unlooked for, unremembered."

Further down in verses 3-5, "God, if I've done what they say- betrayed my friends, ripped off my enemies- If my hands are really that dirty, let them get me, walk all over me, leave me flat on my face in the dirt." Here David is saying, God they will rip me to shreds if they catch me. When a soul has been fragmented, that is just what the enemy does once he has gained access in this manner. He begins to cause emotional pain, confusion, depression and oppression.

Remember that glass vase that has been shattered on the concrete floor, slivers and jagged pieces everywhere. The vase had an intended use when it was created. But now it cannot contain what it once was created to contain, for it is no longer whole. It now resembles a jumbled up jig saw puzzle that has been dumped out by someone, in hopes of being able to put all the pieces back together in their right place.

There Is a Healer

Healing must come to the soul that has been broken and fragmented. This must happen before you can effectively maintain a stance of the front lines. As long as you are fragmented, you have too many in routes for the enemy. And you will find victories are short lived and far in between. Because the battle within your own soul is working against you.

The other reason healing must come is so that the fragmented condition of the soul does not hinder or impair the Spirit of God's ability to arise in your depths as well as rule and reign over the soul. Soul fragmentation is a weapon that the enemy has fashioned to keep the soul from knowing its proper role. As long as the soul is broken and wounded, it will speak louder than the Spirit of God in your life. And the Spirit of God should be the one leading you and not your soul dictating to the Spirit of God.

Another reason the enemy chooses soul fragmentation as a ways to hinder is that it keeps the victim at a place of being impoverished in their soul and spirit. Some are even so fragmented that they seem addicted to the ungodly soul ties that keep them fragmented and broken. For their thinking processes that cause them to choose what is right from wrong for them in regards to a relationship that will cause them to endure additional harm or not has been impaired.

If the person with an ungodly soul tie chooses not to sever the tie 100% and break all communications and contact with this person, the tie is not broken. Restoration to the soul cannot happen for the tie has not been broken completely. This is a real issue for people who have been in abusive, toxic and or idolatrous relationship. People can even in some cases become addicted to the person that they have an ungodly soul tie with that they refuse to sever. This addiction can form such a soul tie that perverts the will of the person as a form of witchcraft. Unless they choose to make a stand and sever all contact, and resist the temptations, they will make a step or two forward- but that soul tie will keep them returning like a dog returning to its vomit. Deliverance for such a person will truly be accomplished when they make up their mind to sever the tie and resist the seductions of the enemy that come via fiery darts that are launched to keep them reminded of what they think they can't live without. Usually the person has suffered great rejection and abandonment which has opened them up to the occult attempting to transform their minds- in order to conform them to a demonic image. These people will always be crying out as a victim, when in reality they will instigate division and destruction if they cannot control the one that they have an ungodly soul tie with. Driven by the addiction that is not getting fed- so to speak. Because if the one person they are addicted to is not responding and reciprocating in their attention, the cravings grow stronger. And like a drug addict in search of a fix when they do not have their craving satisfied- they can endure a breakdown in all arenas- mind, body, soul and spirit. Thus they will become not just manipulative- because the act of controlling the person into submission is not working; but they will become now hostile as well. Sadly I have seen this take place in Churches- where there has been co-dependency with leadership that has led to ungodly soul-ties.

No matter what the cause of the soul fragmentation, there is a healer. We need to seek God for our own personal wholeness. Especially if we are called to restore people and Nations. We cannot lead people somewhere we have not been ourselves. Preaching and praying about restorations is one thing, but we need to have encountered it ourselves, in our own depths, so we can lead others to those waters that restore their soul.

If you are one that is suffering from soul fragmentation, I stand with you in prayer and I agree with you and declare over you that you are every wit whole. That the Spirit of God will gather all the pieces of your broken, fragmented soul and cause wholeness in your soul to be a reality. I declare restoration to you in Jesus Name, so that you can go forth as a vessel of restoration unto people and Nations- for His Glory and His Name Sake, in Jesus Name!

Be Free!

The steps to becoming whole again:
1.   Repent of any actions, words or thoughts that may have contributed to your own soul fragmentation.
2.   Sever in prayer and denounce ever ungodly soul tie. Do what it is necessary in regard to the relationship to the person in the natural to ensure the connection is broken, or brought into proper order.
3.   Forgive yourself and all others who may have contributed to your present condition.
4.   Begin to seek God and declare the Word of God over yourself concerning your wholeness and healing. Allow God To minister healing to the brokenness and make you whole again- restored.

5.
Rebuilding the Walls of Your Life

One Block at a Time

      Spirit of God wants us to reach a place of not being vulnerable to the enemies' attacks. So we can engage in rebuilding the walls around Cities and Nations. In order to accomplish this we must first deal with self.

      In the last sections I dealt with the walls of protection that we erect that are not the walls of protection that God erects to protect us. Also I as well touched on soul fragmentation- our own walls being as rubble. The walls of protection that we erect are based on self-preservation and are not the defenses that we need to guard us from the enemy of our soul. But in fact at times resists the Spirit of God and his help as well as healing.

      The walls of protection that we erect in these circumstances are built with the bricks and mortar of lies, hurts, wounds, bitterness, unforgiveness, anger, pride. As well as countless other issues and spiritual hindrances that come to cause us conflict and trauma. These must be dismantled, so that the hedge of God is restored and we are truly protected from the sniper fire of the enemy.

      On the other hand, you could be one that is just numb from the warfare. You have not took the time nor the energy to build up walls as a defense. Basically you have become an unwalled city lacking discipline and self-control. You have lost hope in your future and grown weary in the battle. Seemingly lost vision, and perishing inwardly. Proverbs 29:18 (AMP) "Where there is no vision (no redemptive revelation of God) the people perish; but he who keeps the law (of God which includes that of man) - blessed (happy, fortunate, and enviable) is he." In either case there is a much needed season of rebuilding and restoring.

Where there once was a brick in your wall labeled pain, it is replaced with healing. Once there was a brick in your wall named hopelessness, and now there is hope. With each exchange that you make, you become stronger as well as restored. If you are unwalled, and desolate, you must grab ahold of hope. Your walls are coming up, the ones that make you a fortified City. Your gates will be restored and opened wide- for the King of Glory to come forth.

If you think back and look back you can see where the enemy has messed and what he has targeted in your life. That's where your restoration should begin. This requires for you to purpose in your heart to be a wise master builder. Apostle Paul states in 1 Corinthians the importance of building skillfully, 3:10 (AMP) "According to the grace (the special endowment for my task) of God bestowed on me, like a skillful architect and master builder I laid (the) foundation, and now another (man) is building upon it. But let each (man) be careful how he builds upon it."

Take an evaluation of yourself and make a list. Have you any residual pain and wounding lingering in your soul? Is there a brick in your wall labeled rejection, betrayal, strife, pride, insecurity? Declare these bricks are removed, and that the answers found in God's Word which are His promises to you replace them. Jeremiah 1: 10 (AMP) "See, I have this day appointed you to the oversight of the nations and of the kingdoms to root out and pull down, to destroy and to overthrow, to build and to plant."

There are some very important building blocks/ bricks that we need to be a part of our walls that are being built. These elements that I will recommend will equip you to be more stable as a Christian and more apt to stand against the wiles of the enemy. Find scriptures that help you build these walls in your life. Seek the revelation that you personally in regards to each point.

The Building Blocks I recommend:

1. Understand who you are in Christ. Deal with insecurities and any confusions as to your identity in Christ.
2. Learn how to hear the voice of God. Deal with issues that block your spiritual senses, including hearing. Confront any internal issues that will cause regret or a guilty conscience.
3. Delivered from every assignment and hindrance of the enemy. Confront the spiritual forces that caused you to erect self-preservation walls. Enter into a time of deliverance from every harassing spirit that has plagued your life. Seek counsel for assistance in this if need be. I recommend your Pastors or Leaders.
4. Know & Understand your spiritual authority as well as what it means to be one under authority.
5. Learn what it means to walk in the Spirit, as well as how to apply the Word of God to your life.
6. Relationship with God. This is a key, and it must be cultivated and developed. Times of intimacy and worship, encountering His presence. Allowing the Spirit of God to speak to you and minister to your heart. Talk to God, conversing with him as you would anyone else.
7. Praise & Worship God, offer Thanksgiving to Him, no matter what. Give God your crazy praise when it just don't make any sense.
8. Healed & whole from old wounds of the past. Including emotional, spiritual, and in the depths of our soul; no more soul fragmentation.
9. Discover your spiritual gifts and how to use them. So you will be secure in the weapons of war that God has equipped you with. As well as skilled in their use.
10. Deliverance from all Generational issues, curses, and ungodly soul ties.
11. Develop an understanding and practice of presenting your bodies as a living sacrifice.
12. Understanding that you are seated in heavenly places, and seeing things from God's point of view.
13. Yielding all of who you are and all that you have unto God.
14. Coming to a place of unity with the Spirit of God, in your depths. Come to the place of being in unity and agreement with the Spirit of God in our mind, will and emotions.

15.   Forgiveness to take residence where there may have been at one time been unforgiveness, bitterness, and judgment
16.   Develop and cultivate the mind of Christ that has been given unto us. Pull down every stronghold, thought and imagination that exalts itself against the knowledge of Christ. Challenge every wrong mindset, renew your mind in the Word of God.
17.   Love- We need to be filled with His love to a state of overflow. The world needs us to be vessels of love that are motivated by love and operate in love.
18.   Replace fear, any and all types, with Faith & Trust in God.

The list may seem overwhelming or challenging, but as you begin to attack this list you will find that you are developing a disciplined spiritual lifestyle. Remember being undisciplined will cause you to be as an unwalled city. Wide open for the attacks of the enemy.

This rebuilding is a process and it will take time. You will need to partner with the Holy Spirit and allow him to do in your depths what only God can do. He just needs your surrender, yielding and agreement.

As you allow yourself to be transformed in areas of your life that you need discipline in, healing and or deliverance; you will find that the hedge is up. The walls of security, which causes you to be as a fortified city stand bold and strong. Spirit of the living God is patrolling your borders, the angels of God are encamped around about you as never before. And the glory of God is your rearguard. Isaiah 52:12 (NAS) "But you will not go out in haste, nor will you go as fugitives; For the Lord will go before you, and the God of Israel will be your rear guard." Nahum 1:7 (NAS) "The Lord is good, a stronghold in the day of trouble, and He knows those who take refuge in Him."

Now you are free and secure in God. You have learned how to govern and rule over your own soul. You are now governing as a watchmen over your own soul, and now you can be trusted and released to be a watchmen over Cities & Nations. Revelations 2:26- (KJV) "And he that overcometh, and keepeth my works unto the end, to him will I give power over the nations." Numbers 14: 24 (KJV) "But my servant Caleb, because he had another spirit with him, and hath followed me fully, him will I bring into the land whereinto he went; and his seed shall possess it."

The rebuilding process is a sign of a New Covenant between God and his beloved Sons & Daughters. Let the rebuilding process begin in your own life. Jeremiah 31:4-6 (NIV) "I will build you up again and you will be rebuilt, O Virgin Israel. Again you will take up your tambourines and go out to dance with the joyful. Again you will plant vineyards on the hills of Samaria; the farmers will plant them and enjoy their fruit. There will be a day when watchmen cry out on the hills of Ephraim, Come, let us go up to Zion, to the Lord our God."

A New Covenant, Jeremiah 31:27 (NAS) "Behold days are coming," declares the Lord, "when I will sow the house of Israel and the house of Judah with the seed of man and with the seed of beast. As I have watched over them to pluck up, to break down, to overthrow, to destroy and to bring disaster, so I will watch over them to build and to plant," declares the Lord. In those days they will not say again, the fathers have eaten sour grapes, and the children's teeth are set on edge. But everyone will die for their own iniquity, each man who eats sour grapes, his teeth will be set on edge. Behold the days are coming, declares the Lord, when I will make a new covenant with the house of Israel and the house of Judah, not like the covenant which I made with their fathers in the day I took them by the hand to bring them out of the land if Egypt. My covenant which they broke, although I was a husband to them, declares the Lord. But this is the covenant I will make with the house of Israel after those days, declares the Lord, I will put MY law within them and on their heart I will write it: and I will be their God, and they shall be My people."

Jeremiah 31:38 (NAS) "Behold, days are coming, declares the Lord, when the city will be rebuilt for the Lord from the Tower of Hananel to the Corner Gate."

Zechariah 1: 16-17 (NAS) "Therefore thus says the Lord, "I will return to Jerusalem with compassion; My house will be built in it." Declared the Lord of hosts, "and a measuring line will be stretched over Jerusalem. Again, proclaim, saying, "Thus says the Lord of hosts, "My cities will again overflow with prosperity, and the Lord will again comfort Zion and again choose Jerusalem."

Zechariah 3:2 (NAS) "The Lord said to Satan, "The Lord rebuke you, Satan! Indeed, the Lord who has chosen Jerusalem rebuke you! Is this not a brand plucked from the fire?"

Zephaniah 3:14-20 (NAS) "Shout for joy, O daughter of Zion! Shout in triumph, O Israel! Rejoice and exult with all your heart, O daughter of Jerusalem! The Lord has taken away His judgments against you. He has cleared away your enemies. The King of Israel, the Lord is in your midst; you will fear disaster no more. In that day it will be said to Jerusalem: Do not be afraid, O Zion; do not let your hands fall limp. The Lord your God is in your midst, a victorious warrior. He will exult over you with joy, He will be quiet in His love. He will rejoice over you with shouts of joy. I will gather those who grieve about the appointed feasts- they came from you O Zion; the reproach of exile is a burden on them. Behold I am going to deal at that time with all your oppressors, I will save the lame. And gather the outcast, and I will turn their shame into praise and renown in all the earth. At that time I will bring you in, even at the time when I gather you together; indeed I will give you renown and praise among all the peoples of the earth. When I restore your fortunes before your eyes, says the Lord."

Zechariah 8:3 (NAS) "Thus says the Lord, I will return to Zion and will dwell in the midst of Jerusalem. Then Jerusalem will be called the City of Truth, and the mountain of the Lord of hosts will be called the Holy Mountain."

6.
Nehemiah Project- Strategy- For City & Soul

Phase One- Repentance- Shifting Our Minds

Nehemiah, the name given to the man used by God to bring forth restoration; means consolation of Jehovah. Consolation as well means compassion, which in Hebrew & Greek means womb. Compassion of Jehovah can be as a womb that will birth an individual, group of people or a Nation from the place of devastation and destruction to a place of restoration and rebuilding.

This is why we need to be as Nehemiah in this day and hour, one's that are used by God to release His compassion and birth out a turnaround. Skilled Master builders, rebuilding that which was once devastated. God's restoring of a person, or City illuminates God's power and ability to take what the enemy meant for destruction and turn it into a time of construction. Nehemiah 2:17 (NIV) "Then I said to them, "You see the trouble we are in: Jerusalem lies in ruins, and its gates have been burned with fire. Come, let us rebuild the wall of Jerusalem, and we will no longer be in disgrace."

I firmly believe it is the message of love & compassion that is needed to be heard and released in the earth today. Jeremiah 15:19 (NIV) "Therefore this is what the Lord says: "If you repent, I will restore you that you may serve me: if you utter worthy, not worthless, words, you will be my spokesman." Worthy words, speaking the Good News is what qualifies us to be His spokesman.

We don't need to be the one trumpeting the message of judgment and wrath, doom and gloom. Causing people to develop a negative mindset of- this is what you should expect to endure and then you die. People are already in a battle to hold onto their hope especially while they are endure suffering. If, because of compassion Jesus physically healed them all, can it not be so for Cities & Nations? Or better yet an impoverished or wayward soul? Matthew 14:14 (NIV) "When Jesus landed and saw a large crowd, he had compassion on them and healed their sick."

Jesus is our example, and if He was moved with compassion and brought healing, are we not to as well be moved with compassion and release healing? Nehemiah the one who carried a burden for a people and a City was not moved to judgment or being critical, nor did he act as if their condition was their own fault. No, he was moved to compassion, he showed mercy and love and became a womb that brought restoration to a people and a City.

Prophetic people have to be mature and not so quick to call down fire and judgment, when the goodness of God can draw people to repentance as well. There may be in fact a need for repentance and correction, orchestrated by the love, mercy and compassion of God. Which can go forth and bring alignment in such a way that people will draw close to God and His glory will be released in a greater measure. Romans 2:4 (Amp) "4 Or are you [so blind as to] trifle with and presume upon and despise and underestimate the wealth of His kindness and forbearance and long-suffering patience? Are you unmindful or actually ignorant [of the fact] that God's kindness is intended to lead you to repent (to change your mind and inner man to accept God's will)?" Ephesians 2:4 "But God, who is rich in mercy, for his great love wherewith he loved us."

Mercy of course was extended by God and even through Nehemiah, a mere cupbearer, servant of the king. Of course mercy is help or assistance given to someone who is in desperate need. In Hebrew & Greek mercy means; favor, kindness, compassion, or womb. We see by these interpretations that mercy is as well a form of compassion which is as a womb birthing someone from a place of need and or darkness to a place of need fulfilled and coming into the light. Lamentations 3:22-23 "It is of the LORD's mercies that we are not consumed, because his compassions fail not. They are new every morning: great is thy faithfulness."

Mercy of God is the compassion of God released that births miracles. We have this example in blind Bartimaeus, Mark 10:47 (NAS) "When he heard that it was Jesus the Nazarene, he began to cry out and say, "Jesus, Son of David, have mercy on me!" Bartimaeus was blinded from birth as was his father. He cried out to Jesus for mercy to be extended to release him not just from blindness and infirmity, but a generational curse. Immediately Bartimaeus was healed as his faith reached out and connected with the mercy and compassion of Jesus.

Romans 9:22-23 (NIV) "What if God, choosing to show his wrath and make his power known, bore with great patience the objects of his wrath- prepared for destruction? What if he did this to make the riches of his glory known to the objects of his mercy, whom he prepared in advance for glory-"

Souls, lives, as well as Nations need to experience the compassion and mercy of God. This is the day and hour we hear so much about grace, but mercy needs to prevail greatly as well. Grace is unmerited favor, we get what we don't deserve. Mercy is extended so that we do not get the punishment that we deserve. James 2:13 (NIV) "because judgment without mercy will be shown to anyone who has not been merciful. Mercy triumphs over judgment!" Proverbs 28: 13 (NIV) "He who conceals his sins does not prosper, but whoever confesses and renounces them finds mercy." We can partake of the benefits of grace and mercy because of the blood of Jesus.

As Sons of God we have been redeemed from getting what we really deserve. Grace is as the intercessor that stands in the gap where judgment is deserved and releases favor. Mercy once released, is the conqueror that triumphs over the judgment. Isaiah 63:9 (NAS) "In all their affliction He was afflicted, and the angel of His presence saved them; In His love and in His mercy He redeemed them, and He lifted them and carried them all the days of old." Hosea 6:6 (NIV) "For I desire mercy, not sacrifice, and acknowledgement of God rather than burnt offerings." Micah 6:8 (NIV) "He has showed you, O, man, what is good. And what does the Lord require of you? To act justly and to love mercy and to walk humbly with our God." Micah 7:18 (NIV) "Who is a God like you, who pardons sin and forgives the transgression of the remnant of his inheritance? You do not stay angry forever but delight to show mercy." Zechariah 1:16 (NIV) "Therefore, this is what the Lord says; 'I will return to Jerusalem with mercy, and there my house will be rebuilt. And the measuring line will be stretched out over Jerusalem,' declares the Lord Almighty."

Nehemiah tapped into grace, as he cried out for mercy, and received favor to go forth and do what he felt the burden of the Lord was leading him to do. Also he became a vehicle to release the mercy of God, because he was filled with compassion for the City. Not only did he feel the burden for the City as an environment and residence, but he as well had compassion for the people that lived in a broken society.

Your Condition Affects Your Position

Nehemiah entered into a time of repentance and soul searching, he began to cry out to God for His mercy to be released. He stood in the gap believing for a pardon for the people as well as the city that had suffered much devastation. For some, repentance needs to start in their own hearts. Because they have endured such hardness that has cultivated bitterness and a harsh attitude. This provokes a critical spirit and a judgmental attitude.

If you are in a bitter and judgmental condition you cannot possibly be used by God to release restoration to a people and or a city. For what lies deep within will manifest as you go forth assisting in the restoration process. Eventually that old way of thinking and those negative emotions will surface and contradict the very work that you are standing in the gap to achieve. This inward heart attitude disqualifies a person from being a womb of compassion that births a turn around and a change. James 2(NIV) "12 Speak and act as those who are going to be judged by the law that gives freedom, 13 because judgment without mercy will be shown to anyone who has not been merciful. Mercy triumphs over judgment."

I am remembering Jonah, who was upset that destruction did not fall on Nineveh because they heeded the Word of the Lord and repented. Jonah 3 (NIV) "8 But let man and beast be covered with sackcloth. Let everyone call urgently on God. Let them give up their evil ways and their violence. 9 Who knows? God may relent and with compassion turn from his fierce anger so that we will not perish. 10 When God saw what they did and how they turned from their evil ways, he had compassion and did not bring upon them the destruction he had threatened."

Turn around took place after heeding the warning and Nineveh repented, Jonah 4 (NIV) "But Jonah was greatly displeased and became angry. 2 He prayed to the Lord, "O Lord, is this not what I said when I was still at home? That is why I was so quick to flee to Tarshish. I knew that you are a gracious and compassionate God, slow to anger and abounding in love, a God who relents from sending calamity. 3 Now, O Lord, take away my life, for it is better for me to die than to live."

Jonah who once received God's compassion, mercy was extended to him when he was in the belly of the whale due to his own disobedience and need of repentance. But now he was in utter despair because God did the same for a City and a people marked for destruction. He desired to die rather than live and see mercy granted to a people that he thought deserved the wrath of God.

The mercy that God showed Nineveh and even Jonah who rebelled against God and the assignment God given to him, is a perfect example of the power of compassion of a merciful God. I cringe when I hear believers speaking doom and gloom over America. When we serve a loving, merciful God that would rather show us compassion than wrath. In regards to Nineveh, we see that God relented, changed His mind about what he intended to do because a people heeded the Word of the Lord and repented.

The people of Nineveh had a change of heart and a change of mind that caused them to have a change in behavior. These changes that they made as they repented changed the heart of God. We serve a God who is no respecter of persons, he did it for Nineveh, and God can do the same for America or any other Nation in crisis. Jonah 4:11 (NIV) "But Nineveh has more than a hundred and twenty thousand people who cannot tell their right hand from their left, and many cattle as well. Should I not be concerned about that great city?" Should God not show compassion and be concerned about your City or this Nation we live in?

We need to of course discern the heart of God concerning people and Nations. But unless the Spirit of God specifically tells you to the contrary, His heart is to release grace and mercy. This is so that through a womb of compassion people and Nations experiencing devastations, shall be birthed into a place of restoration and turn around. But sadly, human nature is not quick to think this way. But the nature of God within us is moved with compassion to bring deliverance and restoration to the people that He loves.

Don't' Be As One of Jobs' Comforters

People and Nations at times undergo hardness and devastations as if the judgment of God has come upon them. And when we as an onlooker see such catastrophes taking place in a Nation or a person's life are we as Job's comforters? Job 4 (NIV) 8"Consider now; who, being innocent, has ever perished? Where were the upright ever destroyed? As I have observed, those who plow evil and those who sow trouble reap it. 9 At the breath of God they are destroyed; at the blast of his anger they perish."

Imagine if you will just for a moment how Job must have felt. The anguish, pain, loss; he just lost his family and all that he owned. And now one of his friends basically says if you were innocent and blameless you would not be perishing right now. If you and your family was upright there would be no destruction. His friend also elated that only someone that has sown bad seeds and done wrong, evil, are the only ones that reap it. Matthew 5:45 (NAS) ".. for He causes His sun to rise on the evil and the good, and sends rain on the righteous and unrighteous."

One of the interpretations of mercy is favor. If you look at the life of Nehemiah he had great favor, and he showed great mercy and compassion by undertaking such a great burden. Nehemiah 2 (NIV) "7 I also said to him, "If it pleases the king, may I have letters to the governors of Trans-Euphrates, so that they will provide me safe-conduct until I arrive in Judah? 8 And may I have a letter to Asaph, keeper of the royal park, so he will give me timber to make beams for the gates of the citadel by the temple and for the city wall and for the residence I will occupy?" And because the gracious hand of my God was on me, the king granted my requests.9 So, I went to the governors of Trans-Euphrates and gave them the king's letters. The king had also sent army officers and cavalry with me." Matthew 5:7 "Blessed are the merciful, for they will be shown mercy."

Lets' allow ourselves to take some life lessons from Nehemiah, and not from Jobs' comforters. Allow God to do the inward work needed within you, so that you can be a womb of compassion birthing forth new life. Shift your mind and your thinking processes from being critical and tearing down, to that of one that is uplifting and building. Be a builder, but first you must be a yielder unto the Spirit of God.

7.
Nehemiah's Burden & Prayer

Begins With Repentance

Nehemiah 1 (NIV) 3They said to me, "Those who survived the exile and are back in the province are in great trouble and disgrace. The wall of Jerusalem is broken down, and its gates have been burned with fire."4 When I heard these things, I sat down and wept. For some days I mourned and fasted and prayed before the God of heaven. 5 Then I said: "Lord, the God of heaven, the great and awesome God, who keeps his covenant of love with those who love him and keep his commandments,6 let your ear be attentive and your eyes open to hear the prayer your servant is praying before you day and night for your servants, the people of Israel. I confess the sins we Israelites, including myself and my father's family, have committed against you. 7 We have acted very wickedly toward you. We have not obeyed the commands, decrees and laws you gave your servant Moses. 8 "Remember the instruction you gave your servant Moses, saying, 'If you are unfaithful, I will scatter you among the nations, 9 but if you return to me and obey my commands, then even if your exiled people are at the farthest horizon, I will gather them from there and bring them to the place I have chosen as a dwelling for my Name.'10 "They are your servants and your people, whom you redeemed by your great strength and your mighty hand. 11 Lord, let your ear be attentive to the prayer of this your servant and to the prayer of your servants who delight in revering your name. Give your servant success today by granting him favor in the presence of this man. I was cupbearer to the king."

    Nehemiah felt the burden of the Lord for a people and a City. His first response to the burden was a cry of repentance. A prayer that acknowledged that the people had sinned against God, but also reminded God of His promise to Moses. That if the people returned to God, their first love, there would be a gathering where there previously had been a scattering. And that restoration would take place because of this act of returning to the Lord and seeking Him first. Matthew 6:33 (NLT) "Seek the Kingdom of God above all else, and live righteously, and he will give you everything you need."

Nehemiah had to believe that he was in right standing with God, as well as believe God had called him to do what he was about to undertake. As he prayed he asked God to be attentive to his prayer, he needed an audience with God, communication had to be established. Solomon, is as well an example of a leader that knew his success was based on the mercy of God, 2 Chronicles 6: 19 (NIV) "Yet give attention to your servants prayer and his plea for mercy, O Lord my God. Hear the cry and the prayer that your servant is praying in your presence."

There needed to be a direct line, no hindrances between Nehemiah and God that interfered with his ability to hear God in order to effectively be guided by God. This is of the upmost importance when you are embarking on an assignment for God. Be sure that you are in right standing and that all hindrances to your Spiritual hearing and being led by the Spirit of God are dealt with and removed. Get all offenses, unforgiveness, judgments, criticalness, anything that could hinder your spiritual senses and gifts from operating these issues must be dealt with. Especially your own thoughts and imaginations. The success of your mission depends on it. 2 Corinthians 10:5 (KJV) "Casting down imaginations, and every high thing that exalteth itself against the knowledge of God, and bringing into captivity every thought to the obedience of Christ." Isaiah 55:8-9 (NAS) "For my thoughts are not your thoughts, nor are your ways My ways, declares the Lord. For as the heavens are higher than the earth, so are My ways higher than your ways and my thoughts than your thoughts."

Beginning to undertake a mandate such as City restoration requires personal soul searching before beginning the journey. There cannot be any doubt, insecurity or jealousy hiding in your depths. You must be secure in who you are in Christ. Know that you are called to this assignment and that if God called you to do it, He will equip you to get through it. Do not lean unto your own understanding. Allow the Mind of Christ to prosper. 2 Corinthians 10 (NIV) "4The weapons we fight with are not the weapons of the world. On the contrary, they have divine power to demolish strongholds. 5 We demolish arguments and every pretension that sets itself up against the knowledge of God, and we take captive every thought to make it obedient to Christ. 6 And we will be ready to punish every act of disobedience, once your obedience is complete."

Take authority over every fear, doubt, or any thought that would come to stop you from moving out into what you have been "SENT" to do. Proverbs 3:5 (NIV) "Trust in the Lord with all your heart and lean not on your own understanding." Psalm 20:7 "Some trust in chariots and some in horses, but we trust in the name of our Lord our God." Psalm 25:1-3 (NIV) "To you, O Lord, I lift up my soul; 2 in you I trust, O my God. Do not let me be put to shame, nor let my enemies triumph over me. 3 No one whose hope is in you will ever be put to shame, but they will be put to shame who are treacherous without excuse."

8.
Unfolding Of the Plan

From Burden to Blueprint

Nehemiah saw the need, and began to allow the burden to impact his heart. All around us are needs, but we will only become a solution if we allow it to burden our heart. Burden, or to be burdened in Hebrew & Greek means; to weigh down, cause pressure, forced labor, authority, task or service, to impose, abundance.

Meditate on the power that is released when you allow a burden to impact your heart and your life. It will weigh you down and cause you to press through and accomplish what is needful to see change. It causes pressure, which makes you uncomfortable and causes you to come out of the place of complacency and come into unity with the Spirit of God and begin to partner with him.

Forced labor, yes it will cause you to work and become busy, active. But it will also impregnate you and cause you to enter into a birthing process that you may not have been looking for and now you suddenly are involved in, forced labor. With the burden of the Lord comes the equipping to fulfill the will of God. Authority will be released to operate in dominion and engage in the process knowing that as you speak all of heaven is backing you up.

A burden from the Lord is nothing short of a task or service that you do as unto the Lord. Carrying a need, a burden in the prayer closet and birthing the answer or intervention from God. I believe it as well means abundance; because with the taking on of a burden, God will release his abundance of what is needed to accomplish what He has assigned you to accomplish. Whether it be favor, provision, money, assistance, no matter what it is God shall abundantly supply.

When you allow yourself to become burdened by the Lord, it impacts your heart. It causes an internal change, a shift in your inward man. Your heart and mind begins to be impacted, you think differently and see differently. Overwhelmed at times by the mercy and compassion of God that says nothing is impossible. Determination rises as you begin to believe now is the time of healing, deliverance, restoration or transformation.

Whatever is needed, the seed-(burden), has been impregnated within the womb-(compassion). And now a birthing process has begun, the birthing of a blueprint and or strategy to bring forth what the burden of the Lord dictates is needed. Transformation began in you, inwardly first, as the burden was implanted in your depths. Then as it was embraced and accepted it was conceived in the womb of compassion.

First stages after the burden has been placed within us of course is repentance. This is why the Spirit of God is dealing so heavily in the areas of renewing the mind- true repentance is to have a Mind Shift- a renewing of the mind. Being transformed in the attitude of your mind by the washing by the water of the Word. Because true repentance is not just saying sorry for your wrong doings- but it is to allow a mind shift that provoked a change in direction; a new attitude as well as altitude.

As I stated previously we must search our hearts and prepare them. Make sure that there are only pure motives in doing what we are about to undertake. Another need for repentance is as with Nehemiah, repenting for the people and anything they did knowingly or unknowingly to contribute to the desolation and destruction that has come upon them. Nehemiah 1:6 (NAS) " let Your ear now be attentive and Your eyes open to hear the prayer of your servant which I am praying before You now, day and night, on behalf of the sons of Israel Your servants, confessing the sins of the sons of Israel which we have sinned against You; I and my father's house have sinned."

The burden that Nehemiah carried had penetrated him so deeply that others could see the weight of what he was carrying. Nehemiah 2:2 (NAS) "So the king said to me, "Why is your face sad though you are not sick? This is nothing but sadness of heart." But the king discerning that Nehemiah was troubled was an open door for Nehemiah to share his burden with the king.

God has already released the burden unto Nehemiah and now the favor of God was going before him to ensure he would have provision that he needed to accomplish it. Nehemiah 2:4 (NAS) "Then the king said to me. "What would you request?" So I prayed to the God of heaven." And now the strategy and blueprint unfolds.
Nehemiah 2:5 (NAS) "I said to the king, if it please the king, and if your servant has found favor before you, send me to Judah. To the city of my fathers' tombs, that I may rebuild it." Nehemiah was birthing out and acting upon the burden. This was provoking favor as he responded to the burden of the Lord.

9.
Implementing the Plan

Sending

Nehemiah 2: 7-9 (NAS) "And I said to the king, "If it pleases the king, let letters be given me for the governors of the provinces beyond the River, that they may allow me to pass through until I come to Judah, and a letter to Asaph the keeper of the king's forest, that he may give me timber to make beams for the gates of the fortress which is by the temple, for the wall of the city and for the house to which I will go." And the king granted them to me because the good hand of my God was on me. Then I came to the governors of the provinces beyond the River and gave them the king's letters. Now the king had sent with me officers of the army and horsemen."

Nehemiah now has been "Sent" by the king to fulfill the mission that began as a burden in his heart. If you recall, Nehemiah said to the king, "Send me to Judah to the city of my fathers' tombs, that I may rebuild it." Nehemiah was sent to accomplish this restoration process of a City, it was not his idea. But a burden of the Lord placed on his heart, because it was a burden on the heart of God that was shared with a willing vessel. So, not only was he sent by the earthly king, but the King of Kings.

This is a vital part of the success of strategy as well, are you "Sent" to do this job? There is a difference in filling a vacancy, just doing something because it needs to be done, and someone who has been SENT to accomplish something. This means they have been sought out by the Lord, burdened, commissioned and positioned. Equipped with everything that is needful to accomplish what they have been SENT to do.

If you are operating under the weight of a burden and compassion is being released that brings change, you have been SENT by God. This is an apostolic term that means one is apostolic and has a message, and they carry the authority of the sender (Jesus Christ). They have spent time with God developing his character, because they represent the sender. Their message is one that has been given to them by the sender and do not want their own nature and character to hinder God or his message.

When you are SENT, such as Nehemiah you have authority in that city, Nation, or situation to bring change, Jeremiah 1:10 (NIV) "See, today I appoint you over nations and kingdoms to uproot and tear down, to destroy and overthrow, and to build and to plant." As was stated in Nehemiah 2:5, a sent one is a builder.

Let's look at Moses who was "Sent". In Psalms 105:22, we see a "Sent" one will teach, "to instruct his princes as he pleased and teach his elders wisdom." As well as heal the sick and cast out devils, signs & wonders & deliverance as referenced as well in Psalms 105: 26-27 "He sent Moses his servant: and Aaron whom he had chosen. They showed his signs among them, and wonders in the land of Ham."

When it comes to rebuilding and restoring lives and cities you must know who you are in Christ and that you are "SENT" to do what you are attempting to do. It will take signs & wonders, the supernatural empowerment of the spirit to accomplish the assignment at hand. You will have to come to a new level of partnering with the Holy Spirit. The things needing to be dealt with are supernatural, firstly, and must be dealt with in the spirit before any manifested change can occur in the natural. Ephesians 6:12 (NIV) "For our struggle is not against flesh and blood, but against the rulers, against the authorities, against the spiritual forces of evil in heavenly realms."

I do believe that because we are a Christian, God will honor what we do to bring Him Glory. But I as well believe there is an extra measure of authority upon someone that is "SENT" to accomplish something for the Kingdom of God. I have seen my share of Ministers and Leaders, some I can tell God did not "SEND", but in fact have sent themselves. There is a difference in the weight of Glory upon their lives. Matthew 22:14 (KJV) "For many are called but few are chosen."

There is a difference between someone who gets hurt and leaves a Ministry and decides to prove something to those who hurt them and rejected them. So they decide to head up their own Church or Ministry, from someone who God handpicked to head a particular Ministry or do a particular work or assignment. There will always be struggles whether "SENT" by God or if you have your own ambitions, motives and agendas. The outcome will be different, the glory will be heavier and the anointing will be obvious and not manufactured or faked. It is important to be led by the Spirit of God especially in embarking in these areas of Ministry. We do not want to do Ministry or start a Church without His covering or His anointing and find ourselves outside of His will.

Zeal Can Be Your Friend or Foe

Sometimes I believe the other hindrance is someone moving forward in the things of God out of zeal and or impatience, sending self before their actual time. Maybe God was going to "SEND" them but they got out there ahead of God, using zeal without wisdom. Now they are like a loaded gun firing off, even friendly fire at times because they did not have adequate time learning to shoot properly at the gun range.

It is important that we know in our hearts concerning self as well as others in regards to spiritual positioning. This will take humbling before God and seeking his counsel and wisdom. Be sure we are not someone's second choice, or just being used to fill a vacancy. Also that we are not in our flesh just wanting a position, but that we were created and ordained by God to step into that position as a "SENT" one, anointed and appointed. Acts 1:23-25 (NAS) "So they put forward two men, Joseph called Barsabas (who was also called Justus), and Mathias. And they prayed and said, "You, Lord, who know the hearts of all men, show which one of these two You have chosen to occupy this ministry and apostleship from which Judas turned aside to go to his own place." 1 Samuel 10:1 (NAS)"Then Samuel took the flask of oil, poured it on his head, kissed him and said, "Has not the Lord anointed you a ruler over His inheritance?"

We can glean from the scriptures concerning David as well, who was chosen by God to be king. Samuel was sent by God to anoint David to replace Saul. 1 Samuel 16:1 (AMP) "The Lord said to Samuel, How long will you mourn for Saul, seeing I have rejected him from reigning over Israel? Fill your horn with oil; I will send you to Jesse the Bethlehemite. For I have provided for Myself a king among his sons." 1 Samuel 16:6-7 (AMP) "When they had come, he looked at Eliab (the eldest son) and said, surely the Lord's anointed is before Him. But the Lord said to Samuel, look not on his appearance or at the height of his stature, for I have rejected him. For the Lord sees not as man sees, for man looks on the outward appearance, but the Lord looks on the heart."

If you are "Chosen" and or "SENT" please do not fret as others seem to have their turn at bat, and you keep seemingly getting passed over. David was in the back fields tending sheep, but God knew who He needed and who He had called to fulfill this assignment. All his brothers went before him and the anointing oil that would set apart one as king was not permitted by God to flow on another. It was appointed oil for one destined for the position, the oil would only flow and anoint for service the one that God had chosen. If we would all allow that to become a personal revelation maybe there would not be so much competition and jealousy in the Church.

Any of the brothers could have assumed the position as king, but the anointing would not flow empowering him and being as a sign to others that he was truly a king. 1 Samuel 16: 11-13 (NAS) "Then (he) said to Jesse, are all your sons here? (Jesse) said, there is yet the youngest; he is tending the sheep. Samuel said to Jesse, send for him: for we will not sit down to eat until he is here. Jesse sent and brought him. David had a healthy reddish complexion and beautiful eyes, and was fine looking. The Lord said to Samuel, arise, and anoint him; this is he. Then Samuel took the horn of oil and anointed David in the midst of his brothers; and the Spirit of the Lord came mightily upon David from that day forward."

There is a shift in the land today. You can see the anointing shifting and changing on people's lives. Some that are in their proper timing and doing as they are called to do, it is increasing. For some there is a stripping like Saul, because they have not been obedient. 1 Samuel 15:26-28 (AMP) "And Samuel said to Saul, I will not return with you; for you have rejected the word of the Lord, and the Lord has rejected you from being king over Israel. And as Samuel turned to go away, Saul seized the skirt of Samuel's mantle, and it tore. And Samuel said to him, The Lord has torn the kingdom of Israel from you this day and has given it to a neighbor of yours who is better than you."

We must know that we are "Sent" by God as well as sensing the urgency and need to be obedient unto what God has sent us to do. If Jonah stayed in the belly of the whale, Nineveh may have never repented. Nehemiah had to allow his heart to be burdened, and receive the strategy for rebuilding as well as be obedient unto it. If not, the City possibly would have continued to lie in ruins. At least until God found another vessel he could trust the assignment with.

Saul was God's choice, anointed and appointed as king. But he was not obedient to what God has asked him to do. In fact Saul took it upon himself to make a decision, a choice based on his own thinking and rationale. One which was in rebellion to the plan according to the way that God had relayed it to Saul.

When we begin to operate as a "SENT ONE" we must be obedient to the details and instructions of the one who "SENT" us. If not our outcome will not be as that of Nehemiah who was able to bring restoration and rebuilding to a city. But the end result will be liken to that of Saul, mantle was torn away from him because of disobedience. A legacy was then passed to another to fulfill.

Implementation of the Strategy of a "SENT-ONE" is crucial to all involved, especially the one implementing the strategy. It must be according to God's blueprint so that the glory of God will be seen by all. 1 Kings 6:11-14 (NAS) "Now the word of the Lord came to Solomon saying, "Concerning this house which you are building, if you will walk in my statutes and execute My ordinances and keep all My commandments by walking in them, then I will carry out my word with you which I spoke to David your father. I will dwell among the sons of Israel, and will not forsake my people Israel." So Solomon built the house and finished it."

After it was built according to the blueprint of God; 1 Kings 8: 10-11 (NAS) "It happened that when the priest came from the holy place, the cloud filled the house of the Lord, so that the priests could not stand to minister because of the cloud, for the glory of the Lord filled the house of the Lord, so the priest could not stand to minister because of the cloud, for the glory of the Lord filled the house of the Lord. Them Solomon said, The Lord has said that He would dwell in the thick cloud. I have surely built You a lofty house, a place for your dwelling forever."

We want to be able to say to our King, "I have surely built You a lofty house, a place for your dwelling forever." A place that the Glory of God remained and not just visited. Where are those structures built according to the blueprints of God? Places that become known as the Habitation of the Lord.

10.
Let Us Arise & Build

Hand In Hand

Nehemiah arrived in Jerusalem, and at night he would arise to go forth in the land and inspect the condition of the city. He did not disclose with others the fullness of the plan. I can see him as he journeyed through the land the spirit of God downloading into him more details, strategy, a blueprint for rebuilding.

Sometimes it is a needful aspect of strategy to not disclose to everyone the vision and strategy. You have to discern who really is with you on this assignment and who is being as a spy for the enemy. It is sad to say there are some that have not matured and developed past their own insecurities and jealousies, so when you include them in the revealing of the strategy, the enemy is able to use them to sabotage what you are being led to do. Nehemiah even inspected the city under the cover of night, as to not be seen by everyone.

There are those as well that because they have unresolved jealousy and insecurity and they have not become reconciled with who they are in Christ, will for lack of a better phrase begin to copycat or steal your ideas and strategy. I as well have witnessed this. It is sad on many levels, because the ones who usually are doing it are so anointed and appointed for what God truly has for them. The other thing is they are trying to do something that God may not have called them do. Meanwhile, what they are really called to do is left undone. And if they are not called to do it then the authority and anointing for effectiveness will not be at the same level as one "Sent" by God to accomplish it.

Operating out of alignment can cause friction when a group of people are trying to implement the Vision & strategy of God. This is the day of unity and accomplishing the agenda of God walking hand in hand. God is no respecter of persons, no one is better than another. God is moving in numbers and not the one man shows anymore. But we all must know our place in the Body as well as any given assignment and we must be faithful unto what God has assigned us to do. If we don't know what it is, seek God for that revelation and get busy. Don't fight battles that God never intended for you to fight.

I want to bring to your attention to the fact that it was the third day that Nehemiah began to implement his plans. Nehemiah 2:11-12 (NAS) "So I came to Jerusalem and was there three days. And I arose in the night, I and a few men with me. I did not tell anyone what my God was putting into my mind to do for Jerusalem and there was no animal with me except the animal on which I was riding." He was incognito, no noisy animals, just the one he was riding on. Nehemiah only had a few men with him as he searched out the city and told no one yet what God had placed on his heart to do.

Nehemiah was using wisdom, getting the fullness of the plan from God. He was birthing it out in the spirit before he began telling the people around him that he felt God had placed with him for this assignment. Nehemiah 2:16-17 (NAS) "The officials did not know where I had gone or what I had done; nor had I as yet told the Jews, the priests, the nobles, the officials or the rest who did the work. Then I said to them, "You see the bad situation we are in, that Jerusalem is desolate and its gates burned by fire. Come, let us rebuild the wall of Jerusalem so that we will no longer be a reproach."

This was a plan, and assignment that was bigger than one man and his Ministry unto God. It was going to take a group of people working in unity, co-laboring together as one construction crew. They would all had to come to a place of common ground and lay down any differences or beliefs that could breed strife or division, so that the blueprint of God could be manifested on the earth. Nehemiah 2:18 (NAS) "I told them how the hand of my God had been favorable to me and also about the king's words which he had spoken to me. Then they said, "Let us arise and build." So they put their hands to the good work."

There Will Be Opposition to Your Commission

Of course their labors were met with opposition, but because Nehemiah was in unity with the Spirit of God in such an unshakeable way he was just that "unshakeable". Nehemiah 2:19-20 (NAS) "But when Sanballat the Horonite and Tobiah the Ammonite official, and Geshem the Arab heard it, they mocked us and despised us and said, "What is this thing you are doing? Are you rebelling against the king? So I answered them and said to them, "The God of heaven will give us success; therefore we His servants will arise and build, but you have no portion, right or memorial in Jerusalem."

Sanballat and Tobiah represent spiritual forces that take assignment against and resist apostolic building and restoration. We see as their harassing increases during the stages of building, it is fueled by intimidation. Attempting to get Nehemiah and those alongside of him to stop the rebuilding process and lay down their tools.

As we can read in Nehemiah chapter 3, each section of the wall was being rebuilt by a different family or group of people. How wonderful it would be if the Body of Christ could forget about their doctrines, and come out from behind denominational walls. With a common goal to join together as they did in Jerusalem to rebuild the walls and gates of Jerusalem.

They did so in unity, and obedience to the assignment of God. With no respect of persons or personal beliefs. They did not stand and judge one another or criticize any differences. They were on common ground and there was a cause. That was their objective, and no other agendas but God's prevailed.

I had a vision one time after praying at the State line of Florida. A couple of us were led to go there and place a brick symbolizing the walls of Nehemiah were being rebuilt. That very day there were many intercessors that went all over the city and outskirts of the city and did likewise. Establishing boundaries for prayer.

Then on a second occasion when I was at the state line praying and we were declaring, I began to see a river of gold flowing down the highway. As I was driving back into town this glorious river was constantly ahead of me. The Spirit of God was speaking to my heart on the way back as I continued to see this river of gold flowing along the coast, and down this main highway. I was reminded of Psalms 133, where there is unity there will be a commanded blessing. Psalms 133:1-3 (KJV) "Behold, How good and pleasant it is for brethren to dwell together in unity! It is like the precious ointment upon the head that ran down upon the beard even Aaron's beard: that went down to the skirts of his garments; as the dew of Hermon, and as the dew that descended upon the mountains of Zion: for there the Lord commanded the blessing, even life for evermore."

It will take unity to bring the release of the commanded blessing- the glory of God in our cities, regions, Nations. I heard the spirit of God speak to me as I had yet another open vision. I began to see helicopters, planes, buses of people coming into the city. It was set apart as a city of refuge, a habitation of God. People from everywhere were coming to be healed, delivered, and to receive manifested miracles. All because the glory of God was here in the City and it was as the Temple of Solomon, a habitation that had been built according to God's blueprints and the glory remained.

The spirit of God spoke to me and said explicitly, "This will only happen with unity, I will release this glory as a commanded blessing." This means the revival and the miracles I was witnessing in the Spirit was not just for one or two Churches. I saw it was for all that aligned themselves properly, with Jesus as the head of their Church. Part of the aligning was coming hand in hand with other Ministers and Ministries in the City and rebuilding and believing for the unity that releases the commanded blessing.

Nehemiah is a great example of bringing such as it is in heaven to the earth. He received the blueprint from heaven and he began to rebuild and implement the strategy accordingly. Hand in hand- families, groups, tribes came together as one and they began to rebuild the walls and gates of Jerusalem that had been devastated by the enemy. Their obedience to be unified and work the strategy of heaven, gave them a city that was rebuilt, restored and no longer as an unwalled city open to the attacks of the enemy. Restoration to a City and a people was achieved as they worked hand in hand.

I pray and declare these scriptures concerning Unity over the Body of Christ.

2 Chronicles 30: 12 (NIV) "Also in Judah the hand of God was on the people to give them unity of mind to carry out what the king and his officials had ordered, following the word of the Lord." John 17:23 (NIV) "I in them and you in me. May they be brought to complete unity to let the world know that you sent me and have loved them even as you have loved me?" Romans 15:5-6 (NIV) "May the God who gives endurance and encouragement give you a spirit of unity among yourselves as you follow Christ Jesus, so that with one heart and mouth you may glorify the God and Father of our Lord Jesus Christ." Ephesian 4:3 (NIV) "Make every effort to keep the unity of the Spirit through the bond of peace."

11.
Believe God Will Grant You Success

Your Work Will Be Ridiculed- Birthing Of a Leader

As you probably already know, as you make up your mind to go forward with God, the enemy is strategizing to hinder you. The same was with Nehemiah and his builders. Nehemiah 4: 1-2 (NAS) "Now it came about that when Sanballat heard that we were rebuilding the wall, he became furious and very angry and mocked the Jews. He spoke in the presence of his brothers and the wealthy men of Samaria and said, "What are these feeble Jews doing? Are they going to restore it for themselves? Can they offer sacrifices? Can they finish in a day? Can they revive the stones from the dusty rubble even the burned ones?

The harassers were trying to stop progress and if they could not intimidate Nehemiah they would attempt to influence the wealthy people against him. This is called hitting where it hurts. Many times we have a vision from the Lord and we begin to engage in the process of doing what is required to see it fulfilled and suddenly a financial struggle begins. The enemy is attempting to stop the rebuilding by drying up the funds that it takes to achieve the blueprint you have been given from God.

As leaders we can learn some leadership skills from Nehemiah that will make us more efficient as we oversee building processes. No matter what, he remained confident in God and that this was his building project and God would grant them success no matter what the opposition. He did not despair or get discouraged and emotional. He maintained a right attitude and was a leader that they could follow by example in this building process.

Nehemiah answered the enemies threats and warfare with prayer, Nehemiah 4:4-6 (NAS) "Hear, O our God, how we are despised! Return their reproach on their own heads and give them up for plunder in the land of captivity. Do not forgive their iniquity and let not their sin be blotted out before You, for they have demoralized the builders. So we built the wall and the whole wall was joined together to half its height, for the people had a mind to work."

Part of being a good Leader is the ability to lead others in the midst of rebuilding and warfare. As well as in the midst of it all, having the ability to discern where those on your team are at spiritually. As a leader we must be sensitive to their needs and be able to help them push forward when the enemy bombards them in an attempt to hinder and stop their momentum. This will in the end work to hinder the progress of the project or vision.

If the members in your Church, Ministry or those working with you on an assignment are working at full capacity how much more will they be able to accomplish for the glory of God? They will be more productive and sensitive to the Spirit of God and you will not have to lead them every step of the way. If they are emotionally whole and doing what they know to do in the spirit your job as a leader will be so much easier. They will know what to do accordingly for they are led by the Spirit of God.

In order to maintain that balance, leaders have to be sensitive to those they are connected too. And be quick to minister, pray and speak to those that are under attack or drifting of course. What they do or don't do affects the whole team as well as the assignment. Nehemiah knew this and when discouragement tried to come in the camp, he confronted it immediately.

Take note of Nehemiah's leadership skills in these passages: Nehemiah 4:9-20 (NAS) "But we prayed to our God, and because of them we set up a guard against them day and night. Thus in Judah it was said, 'The strength of the burden bearers is failing, yet there is much rubbish; and we ourselves are unable to rebuild the wall'. Our enemies said, 'They will not know or see until we come among them, kill them and put a stop to the work.' When the Jews who lived near them came and told us ten times. 'They will come up against us from every place where you may turn,' then I stationed men in the lowest parts of the space behind the wall, the exposed places, and I stationed the people in families with their swords, spears and bows. When I saw their fear, I rose and spoke to the nobles, the officials and the rest of the people: 'Do not be afraid of them; remember the Lord who is great and awesome, and fight for your brothers, your sons, your daughters, your wives and your houses.' When our enemies heard that it was known to us, and that God had frustrated their plan, then all of us returned to the wall, each one to his work. From that day on, half of my servants carried on the work while half of them held the spears, the shields, the bows and breastplates: and the captains were behind the whole house of Judah. Those who were rebuilding the wall and those who carried burdens took their load with one hand doing the work and the other holding a weapon. As for the builders, each wore his sword girded at his side as he built, while the trumpeter stood near me, I said to the nobles, the officials and the rest of the people, 'The work is great and extensive, and we are separated on the wall far from one another. At whatever place you hear the sound of the trumpet, rally to us there. Our God will fight for us."

Nehemiah was wise in warfare as well as rebuilding. He reinforced the people, as well as covered all exposed areas and breeches along the wall that the enemy may try to enter in through. He recognized the discouragement and fear of his people and he quickly spoke to them concerning it. Nehemiah did not allow feelings and emotions, or what he thought and saw in the natural influence his ability to see past the present and keep building and moving forward. He confronted their discouragement and emotional distress, he took authority over it by telling them not to be afraid, trust God and fight for your families.

His example was liken to that which Paul admonished us to be like- Christ like; Philippians 2:1-5 (NAS) "Therefore if there is any encouragement in Christ, if there is any consolation of love, if there is any fellowship of the Spirit, if any affection and compassion, make my joy complete by being of the same mind, maintaining the same love, united in spirit, intent on one purpose. Do nothing from selfish or empty conceit, but with humility of mind regard one another as more important than yourselves; do not merely look out for your own personal interests, but also for the interests of others. Have this attitude in yourselves which was also in Christ Jesus."

As you read the book of Nehemiah you can see the wisdom of Nehemiah to ensure victory. Placing the people strategically along the walls, equipping them with swords as well as building tools. This is representative of the fact that as you engage in rebuilding, it is warfare. Continually eluding to the fact that no matter what, God will show them success, for He is fighting for them.

Nehemiah- a Diligent Leader

Nehemiah is an example of Leadership in the midst of warfare and rebuilding. He always stayed above any emotional reactions. His focus remained on the assignment at hand, no matter what the opposition. His confidence was in God and His ability to see them through to completion. His motto could have been, Philippians 1:6 (NAS) "For I am confident of this very thing, that He who begun a good work in you will perfect it until the day of Christ Jesus."

Nehemiah was a leader that they could follow into combat as well as restoring a city. In Romans 12:8 we are charged to be diligent in whatever our gift and calling is, " if it is encouraging let him encourage; if it is contributing to the needs of others, let him give generously; if it is leadership let him govern diligently; if it is showing mercy let him do it cheerfully." Nehemiah was a diligent leader.

Though the enemy strategized against them and mocked what they were doing, these things did not move Nehemiah from his stance nor his assignment. Even when the warfare became more personally threatening. False accusations and a plot to kill him emerged as an attempt to stop him because nothing else was able to stop him or the rebuilding.

Nehemiah 6:5-16 (NAS) "Then Sanballat sent his servant to me in the same manner a fifth time with an open letter in his hand. In it was written, 'It is reported among the nations, and Gashmu says, that you and the Jews are planning to rebel; therefore you are rebuilding the wall. And you are to be their king, according to these reports. You also appointed prophets to proclaim in Jerusalem concerning you, 'A king is in Judah!' And now it will be reported to the king according to these reports. So come now, let us make counsel together.' Then I sent a message to him saying, 'Such things as you are saying have not been done, but you are inventing them in your own mind.' For all of them were trying to frighten us, thinking, 'they will become discouraged with the work and it will not be done.' But now O God, strengthen my hands. When I entered the house of Shemaiah the son of Delaiah, son of Mehetabel, who was confined at home, he said, 'Let us meet together in the house of God, within the temple, and let us close the doors of the temple, for they are coming to kill you, and they are coming to kill you at night.' But I said,

'Should a man like me flee? And could one such as I go into the temple to save his life? I will not go in.' Then, I perceived that surely God had not sent him, but he uttered his prophecy against me because Tobiah and Sanballat had hired him. He was hired for this reason that I might become frightened and act accordingly and sin, so that they might have an evil report in order that they could reproach me. Remember, O my God, Tobiah and Sanballat according to these works of theirs, and also Noadiah the prophetess and the rest of the prophets who were trying to frighten me. So the wall was completed on the twenty-fifth of the month Elul, in fifty-two days. When all our enemies heard of it, and all the nations surrounding us saw it, they lost their confidence; for they recognized that this work had been accomplished with the help of our God."

When all other attempts to stop Nehemiah failed, then it became personal. In a last ditch effort the enemy attempted to use character assassination. Doing so, the enemy hoped that Nehemiah would be afflicted enough to become emotional and react out of his flesh towards those who were being used by the enemy of his soul. Proverbs 2:7-8 (NIV) "He holds victory in store for the upright, he is a shield to those whose walk is blameless, for he guards the course of the just and protects the way of his faithful ones."

This plot they conspired using even a prophetess and other prophets against Nehemiah reminds me of Jezebel opposing Naboth. Jezebel conspires in ways that bring a character assassination in hopes of positioning one in a place of vulnerability in order to steal their land. Naboth refused to give Ahab his land, his inheritance so Jezebel conspired against him. 1 Kings 21:11-16 (NIV) "So the elders and nobles who lived in Naboth's city did as Jezebel directed in the letters she had written to them. They proclaimed a fast and seated Naboth in a prominent place among the people. Then two scoundrels came and sat opposite him and brought charges against Naboth before the people, saying, "Naboth has cursed both God and the king." So they took him outside the city and stoned him to death. Then they sent word to Jezebel: "Naboth has been stoned and is dead." As soon as Jezebel heard that Naboth had been stoned to death, she said to Ahab, "Get up and take possession of the vineyard of Naboth the Jezreelite that he refused to sell you. He is no longer alive, but dead, he got up and went down to take possession of Naboth's vineyard."

I see this so often in the Body of Christ, sadly. Prophetic people need to be sure that they are not being manipulated by others and especially by spiritual forces to prophecy against the brethren based on personal agendas and or thoughts and imaginations. That's why we are instructed, 2 Corinthians 10: 4-5 (KJV) "(For the weapons of our warfare are not carnal, but mighty through God to the pulling down of strongholds ;) Casting down imaginations, and every high thing that exalteth itself against the knowledge of God, and bringing into captivity every thought to the obedience of Christ;"

We need to remember the scriptures concerning Balaam & Balak, whether we are one that is facing an attack of character assassination or the one that feels justified in initiating one against another. Numbers 22:10-12 (NIV) "Balaam said to God, "Balak son of Zippor, king of Moab, sent me this message: A people that has come out of Egypt covers the face of the land. Now come and put a curse on them for me. Perhaps then I will be able to fight them and drive them away." But God said to Balaam, "Do not go with them. You must not put a curse on those people, because they are blessed."

Usually when someone takes charge against you and or the work you are doing for the Lord it is based on jealousy, insecurity, fear that you will succeed and accomplish something or obtain something greater than them and what they have. They feel threatened by you in some way as was the case with Balak, he was fearful of the multitude of people that had been released from Egypt. He was concerned they would take over.

Balak persisted in acquiring the prophetic voice of Balaam to join his cause against these people that he was threatened by. He was very insistent and tried numerous times to convince the Prophet to prophecy against them, curse them. But every time Balaam inquired of God first, he was told not to curse but to bless. This is a valuable lesson for those operating in the prophetic do not let people's opinions or experiences, nor even your own observations cause you to prophesy from that place and not from the spirit.

If you do, you may be guilty of witchcraft/divination. Prophesying curses and judgments unauthorized by God, which originated in your soul under an influence of a demonic spirit known as the accuser of the brethren. And if we are in right standing with God we do not need to fear the words and curses of men. The only way it really can hinder us is if we believe in its power to affect us.

Many people empower by their own words and beliefs, what God in all reality has said shall not be a weapon formed against us. Charismatic circles are notorious for spending time defending themselves from charismatic witchcraft, friendly fire, witchcraft in the pews. Meanwhile the enemy that is causing multitudes to be damned to hell every minute is laughing at us as he drags souls off to his pits by the multitudes.

We forget so quickly what God spoke through Balaam, Numbers 23:18-21 (NIV) "Then he uttered his oracle: "Arise Balak, and listen; hear me son of Zippor. God is not a man, that he should lie, nor a son of man, that he should change his mind. Does he not speak and then not act? Does he promise and not fulfill? I have received a command to bless; he has blessed, and I cannot change it. No misfortune is seen in Jacob, no misery observed in Israel. The Lord their God is with them; the shout of the King is among them."

If you are going to be as a Nehemiah, filled with compassion to be as a womb to birth Cities and people into a state of restoration; you must not allow the words the enemy may speak about you or to you impact you. Listening to the accusers, your opposition, and their curses will cause you to become hardened and bitter as you lean your ear to hear thus saith the devil.

For each time you entertain the witchcraft released against you, you are allowing it to become an effective weapon formed. As you rehearse the lies of the enemy, replay them in your mind, they are defiling you, vexing your soul and you are helping them to prosper against you. If not careful these word curses will embitter you and cause you to be as one that releases judgments against another yourself.

Do not listen to the Balaks in the land. Do not believe in the power of their curses more than the power of God to ensure that they will not affect you, because you are His. For just as God spoke over Israel, the enemy cannot curse what God has blessed. You are blessed because "The shout of the KING is among you."

Sometimes the Key is Agree to Disagree

Sometimes disagreements arise and people believe they have the authority of God and are justified to prophecy the defeat of their brethren. When in fact it's a matter of a personal conflict and not seeing one another's point of view. Next thing we know words are spoken, prayed and declared over another person's life and or Ministry unto God. Romans 14:4 (NIV) "Who are you to judge someone else's servant? To his own master he stands or falls. And he will stand, for the Lord is able to make him stand." Matthew 7:1-2 (NIV) "Do not judge, or you too will be judged. For in the same way you judge others, you will be judged, and with the same measure that you use, it will be measured to you."

We need to be careful in these areas, we could be coming against God himself and what he told a man or woman of God to do. It does not matter if we agree with it or not, God does not need our permission. He is God and he can use whomever and do whatever He chooses. That's why we are told to develop the mind of Christ and possess His thoughts which are higher. Isaiah 55; 9 (KJV) "For as the heavens are higher than the earth, so are my ways higher than yours, and my thoughts than your thoughts."

Once again, Nehemiah past the test. He did not bow or give in even when the attack became personal and he was lied on and about. Nehemiah never forgot his spiritual positioning, Ephesians 2:6 (NIV) "And God raised us up with Christ and seated us with him in the heavenly realms in Christ Jesus." He knew that he had a choice as well as a responsibility. The choice was to walk worthy of his calling even in the face of personal conflict and opposition. Philippians 1:27-28(NAS) "Only conduct yourselves in a manner worthy of the gospel of Christ, so that whether I come and see you or remain absent, I will hear of you that are standing firm in one spirit, with one mind striving together for the faith of the gospel; in no way alarmed by your opponents- which is a sign of destruction for them, but salvation for you, and that too, from God."

His responsibility was to rebuild Jerusalem and to lead the people with integrity, those assigned with him in the rebuilding process. This can only be accomplished in the midst of warfare and personal conflict by choosing to walk in the spirit no matter what. I John 2:6 (NIV) "Whoever claims to live in him must walk as Jesus did."

The walls and gates were rebuilt, as scripture says the people had a mind to work. This mind to work and the flow of unity was inspired from the head down. Remember the saying as the head goes, so does the body. Leaders, we must be in unity within ourselves with the Spirit of God. As well as be as Joshua and Caleb, positioned to possess the Promised Land. Numbers 14:24 (NIV) "But because my servant Caleb has a different spirit and follows me wholeheartedly, I will bring him into the land he went to, and his descendants will inherit it."

Caleb had a different mindset, not one of a victim but a victor. He believed God had given them the land as a promise and he believed that as an infallible truth more than any opposition that stood before them. So as did Nehemiah, he was a persistent and diligent leader. This enabled him to accomplish and complete the assignment of rebuilding Jerusalem.

Having a dream, vision, assignment from God is just the beginning. There is individual preparing as well as the preparation and unifying of those who will be a part of the implementing and fulfilling of the assignment and or vision. Nehemiah was a leader, and by his example, I can see areas that truly I as well can develop in. Because the Kingdom of God is at hand and we should aspire to become a more diligent, successful leader.

Being able to hear, "Well done, my good and faithful servant", is what I long to hear. I desire to be as Nehemiah, heart full of compassion that allows a burden of the Lord to be birthed into a blueprint. A leader that no matter what the opposition I am sensitive to those who are a part of my team. And I am an example of what to do for the glory of God in the face of opposition.

12.
The Gates Need To Be Restored

Spirit of God, as soon as I opened my eyes this morning, spoke to me go and revise "The Nehemiah Project." As I was reviewing, he began to minister to me about the gates- spiritual gates that need to be restored. A gate in Hebrew and Greek means- a door, an entranceway- an opening, a gateway. Gates are strategic openings and even portals into new realms and territories. In the biblical times of the Old Testament especially- we see many accounts, when a king passed through the gate, that king was able to possess that City that was beyond that Gate. Much warfare was conducted at the gates of a stronghold or a city, because if the gate was overrun by the enemy, and the opposing king was able to enter in- the opposition would then take captive- take possession of that land that was being contended for.

2 Chronicles 25:23 "Then Joash king of Israel captured Amaziah the king of Judah, the son of Joash the son of Jehoahaz at Bethshemesh, and brought him to Jerusalem from the Gate of Ephraim to the corner gate of 400 cubits."

Acts 9:24 "but their plot became known to Saul. They were also watching the gates day and night so that they might put him to death."

We need to examine that in the Spirit, if the demonic oppressors enter our gates, and make the way for the strongman- the king; to enter in- then we have war in our borders as the enemy of our soul is attempting to take possession of our gates and our land. Our eyes, ears and mouth are crucial gates to our own soul, that we often neglect being as a watchman over; then we find ourselves in turmoil and warfare in our own depths because what we allowed to enter in our own gates. Due to warfare, sometimes our own gates are broken down- so we neglect our duty to as well guard our own souls and land. Jeremiah 51:30 "The mighty men of Babylon have ceased fighting. They stay in the strongholds; their strength is exhausted. They are becoming like women; their dwelling places are set on fire. The bars of her gates are broken." Ezekiel 38:11 ".. and you will say, 'I will go up against the land of unwalled villages. I will go against those who are at rest, that live securely, all of them living without walls and having no bars nor gates." The land and people with no gates, stand to be a people and a land that is overrun by the enemy.

There are so many Biblical examples of gates- and they all have specific purposes. In Genesis 22:17 we see the Capturing Gate- "Indeed I will greatly bless you, and I will greatly multiply your seed as the starts of the heavens and as the sand which is on the seashore, and your seed shall possess the gates of their enemy." This is an example of a gateway opened by the Lord that took Abraham to a land of promise and that released a generational blessing.

Nehemiah's journey began as a burden planted in his heart by the knowledge that the gates were burned down and the walls of the city were destroyed; thus the people were being overrun; Nehemiah 1:3 "They said to me, 'The remnant there in the province who survived the captivity are in great distress and reproach, and the wall of Jerusalem is broken down and its gates are burned with fire." Nehemiah became heart sick over the condition of the gates; they were burned down and now the people were vulnerable to attacks, and their lives were in ruins.

Can you not as well sense this is prophetic for the heart of the Father and his compassion that he has for us- his people. Our gates are burned down, our walls are in some cases non-existent; making us vulnerable to the dictates and pillaging of the enemy. When he desires us to experience- Zechariah 2:5 "And I myself will be a wall of fire around it, declares the Lord, and I will be its glory within." When we engage in restoring our walls, and the rubble removed- we are coming into agreement with the spirit of God by removing every hindrance and opposition in our lives that keeps us from being totally surrendered and in unity with the Spirit of God. The hedge goes up, the commanded blessing for unity with God- "He becomes a wall of fire around us". Preparing us for- "and I will be its glory within."

Psalm 24:7-9 "Lift up your heads, O gates, and be lifted up, O ancient doors. That the King of glory may come in! Who is the King of glory? The Lord strong and mighty. The Lord mighty in battle. Lift up your heads, O gates, and lift them up, O ancient doors. That the King of glory may come in."

Like I mentioned earlier whichever King emerges thru the gates- is the one that takes possession and rules over the land. When we decide to allow the Spirit of God to take control and sit on the throne of our lives- we will begin to see an inner restoration. As we begin to experience restoration of our soul, our gates will be rebuilt, the walls that were once broken, that made us as an unwalled city- open to the enemies trespasses; will now be erected. And to ensure no more hostile take overs by the enemy; as long as we engage in remaining in unity with the Spirit of God- the King of Glory will come in , in a new way- and possess our gates as well as the land beyond the gates. He will sit on the throne of our hearts as the King of Kings and our soulish man and its emotions and thoughts- will take its proper role in servitude to the King that now possesses the land.

How can we effectively restore gates and walls in territories and Nations, when we ourselves are continually being overrun by the wiles of the enemy; any and every firey dart of the enemy knocks us off the wall of our soul? Then we become overrun and undone, we have not mastered being a watchmen over our soul; we are not ready to be a watchmen over Nations.

Let us now begin the Prophetic Journey of the walls of Jerusalem that were referenced in Nehemiah being restored. 3:1-8: 'Then Eliashib the high priest arose with his brothers the priests and built the Sheep Gate; they consecrated it and hung its doors. Now the sons of Hassenaah built the Fish Gate; they laid its beams and hung its doors with its bolts and bars. And next to them Meremoth the son of Uriah the son of Hakkoz made repairs. And next to him Meshullam the son of Berechiah the son of Meshezabel made repairs. And Joiada the son of Paseah and Meshullam the son of Besodeiah repaired the Old Gate; they laid its beams and hung its doors, with its bolts and its bars. And next to him Hananiah, one of the perfumers, made repairs, and they restored Jerusalem as far as the Broad Wall.'

If you note, even in this restoration process; Nehemiah may have had the vision- but the restoration would have never taken place if he attempted to accomplish it on his own. There will not be any successful one man shows or kingdoms made unto the glory of man- soon coming. We better recognize God is speaking in the spirit and he is break down every wall that keeps you separated and isolated; it is time to link arms with your brethren- time to get this thing built.

The very first gate that was restored was the sheep gate- by which the sacrificial sheep and lambs were brought in. This is the beginning of our journey as we surrender our lives unto the Lamb of God. We honor his life given as a sacrifice as we in return do so likewise. John 15:13 "Greater love hath no man than this than a man lay down his life for his friends." 1 John 3:16 "This is how we know what love is; Jesus Christ laid down his life for us. And we ought to lay down our lives for our brothers and sisters." This speaks to me as well as the place that the sheep have a heart check- our motivations for what we do. So many today do not lay their lives down for one another out of love, but for what is in it for them. They are building their own throne and their own kingdom and they will use and abuse people if need be to accomplish it. They will steal the people of God's money by perverting the holy act of taking up tithes and offering; for their own selfish gain. Body of Christ, we need the Sheep gate restored so that we can begin again- with a right heart and a right mind; and once again we lay our lives down for our God and the brethren as an act of true- pure love, with no thought of self or what we can gain. We need some goats to make another pass through the Sheep Gate. Romans 12:1 "Therefore, I urge you, brothers and sisters, in view of God's mercy, to offer your bodies as a living sacrifice, holy and pleasing to God- this is your true and proper worship."

The Sheep Gate is as well symbolic for where the journey begins, everything we endure after this point all originated from our first encounter- passing through this gate. We need to restore the Sheep gate, we need to repair it and prepare for the harvest that is to come. Some, have lost their first love, and have grown cold. Revelation 2:4 "But I have this against you that you have abandoned your first love."

We are about to see the greatest harvest ever- we must repair the Gateway that they shall come through. Matthew 7:13 "Enter you in at the strait gate; for wide is the gate, and broad is the way, that leads to destruction, and many there be which go in thereat:" Matthew 9:37 "Then he said to his disciples, 'The harvest is plentiful but the workers are few." Too many goats- that have lost the vision of what Christianity is really about- souls. We need to see the Sheep Gate restored, and the rebirthing of the fire of evangelism. This will be a hearkening for the Evangelist to Arise!

The next gate restored was then the Fish Gate. This was called the Fish Gate because this is where the fishermen of Galilee came through this gate to sell their fish that they caught. Now, that the purifying and the returning to God- or the birthing forth and laying down the lives of the Sheep has taken place; now we have evangelism. This is why we haven't seen such a fire and passion for Evangelism- the gate way- the entranceway or portal of release that thrusts those out into the fields of harvest has been destroyed, and in some cases some are just stuck at the Sheep Gate; because they have not fully transformed unto the nature and identity of a Sheep- made in the image of the Lamb of God. This is why the fields are ripened and ready for harvest, but the laborers are few. But the compassion of God is being released and these gates and the lives surrounding them shall be restored- for God's plans and purposes.
Matthew 4:19 "Come, follow me,' Jesus said, and I will send you out to fish for people."
Mark 1:17 "And Jesus said unto them, Come ye after me, and I will make you to become fishers of men."

The next gate rebuilt was the Old Gate- in Nehemiah this is the only place you find reference to an Old Gate. It may have been one of the oldest and or original gates. But it clearly speaks of a restoring of the old, ancient paths and truths that have seemed to have been drowned out by all the new. Hardly do we hear messages of hell even though we need to be reminded that there is a heaven to gain and a hell to shun. Messages on the Holy Spirit, the blood, faith, mercy and love; all these foundational truths that sometimes we just need to revisit and be reminded of. For as I said they are our foundation that we stand on.
Jeremiah 6:16 "This is what the Lord says: 'Stand at the crossroads and look; ask for the ancient paths, ask where the good way is, and walk in it and you will find rest for your souls. But you said, we will not walk in it."

The next Gate restored was the Valley Gate- this speaks of the trials that birthed perseverance and strength in us. The valley is where we grow, but so many want to escape these growing experiences and times- they want to find an escape route. We are truly spoiled, we want microwave Christianity- instant in the heat of adversity and right back out. With each valley there is a lesson to learn, change that takes place in our midst- it is these trials and sufferings that qualify us for the weight of glory that is to come.

The thing about a Gate especially the Valley Gate- it is an entranceway that usually had a path beyond the entranceway that took you through something. Not like the wilderness that had no straight cut path to the other side, but instead you go around and around in your circumstance- carving out ruts for feet by traveling the same path over and over- religiously bound to this familiar path that does not lead to change. Many battles are fought and many kings were destroyed in the valleys of the Old Testament scriptures, here we have a picture of the battles waged and won in the valley.

Isaiah 40:3-4 "A voice is calling, 'Clear the way for the Lord in the wilderness; make smooth in the desert a highway for our God. Let every valley be lifted up, and every mountain and hill be made low and let the rough ground become a plain, and the rugged terrain a broad valley."

    The next Gate restored was the Dung Gate- the refuse gate. All of Jerusalem's refuse and rubbish was taken out through the dung gate, down to the valley of Hinnom, where it would be burned. This is where the rubbish is removed and this is what happens in our own life. Valley experiences are used by the Lord to clear away the rubbish so that true faith, refined by the fire, can come forth and produce fruit. Clearing away the rubbish in our lives is never easy but the benefits of this experience can be seen in the next gate. If you were to look geographically on a map as to where this gate was positioned- after this point instead on downward you begin to move upward. Symbolic for a point of your Christian life where there is a dramatic 'turning of the corner' that takes place. Up until this point we have been moving downward and the experiences have been hard, but having come to this point there is a sharp turn in the road and we begin to move upward again. As the load becomes lighter as we loose ourselves from the refuse of life, and separate ourselves from the dung that is as a stench to the nostrils.

Jeremiah 15:19 "Therefore, thus says the Lord, 'If you return, then I will restore you- Before Me you will stand; and if you extract the precious from the worthless, you will become my spokesman. They for their part may turn to you, but as for you, you must not turn to them."

Malachi 3:2-4 "But who can endure the day of His coming? And who can stand when He appears? For He is like a refiner's fore and like fullers' soap. He will sit as a smelter and purifier of silver, and He will purify the sons of Levi and refine them like gold and silver, so they may present to the Lord offerings in righteousness. Then the offering of Judah and Jerusalem will be pleasing to the Lord as in the days of old and as in former years."

Job 23:10 "But He knows the way I take; When He has tried me, I shall come forth as gold."

Isaiah 48:10 "Behold, I have refined you, but not as silver; I have tested you in the furnace of affliction."

     The next gate to be restored was the Fountain Gate- The fountain gate is located near the pool of Siloah and was often used by the people for cleaning before proceeding on to the temple. This gate was located extremely close to the dung gate. In other words, after a valley type experience where rubbish in our lives is cleared out through the dung gate, a new life and experience in Christ comes forth and the fountains begin to flow quite quickly! This speaks to us of the living waters of the Holy Spirit that cleanse our lives and empower us for our Christian life. Jesus said: 'Whoever believes in me, as the Scripture has said, streams of living water will flow from within him."(John 7:38)

John 4:14 "But those who drink the water I give will never be thirsty again. It becomes a fresh, bubbling spring within them, giving them eternal life."

     Then we come to the Water Gate and its restoration process. The water gate is a picture of the word of God and its effect in our lives. It is no coincidence that this gate was located next to the fountain gate as the two often go together. The Holy Spirit is the one who makes the word of God alive to us personally, allowing cleansing, encouragement and direction to take place in our life. Being washed by the water of the Word baptizes us into a time of transformation. No longer looking like what we just been through but being conformed to the image of Christ. This is where we will experience some divine exchange, as we allow the Word of God to renew our minds.

Ephesians 5:26 "that He might sanctify and cleanse her with the washing of water by the word."

Revelations 22:17 "The Spirit and the bride say, 'Come'. Let anyone who hears this say, 'Come'. Let anyone who is thirsty come. Let anyone who desires drink freely from the water of life."

The next Gate to be rebuilt us the Horse Gate. The horse gate was close to the King's stables and the men of Jerusalem would ride their horses out of this gate. : The horse gate speaks to us of warfare as horses were used in battle and became a symbol of war, conflict- battle. Example- Revelation 19:11 'I saw Heaven opened, and behold a white horse; and he that sat upon him was called Faithful and True, and in righteousness does He judge and make war.' It is also interesting that the horse gate follows the water (word) gate for as the word goes forth the spiritual warfare is sure to increase!

Ephesians 3:10 "His intent was that now, through the church, the manifold wisdom of God should be made known to the rulers and authorities in the heavenly realms."

The following gate mentioned in the restoration process was the East Gate. The East gate is located on the opposite side of the Mount of Olives. Ezekiel 44:1-3 "... the gate that looked toward the east, and it was shut. The Lord said to me, 'This gate shall be shut; it shall not be opened, and no one shall enter by it, for the Lord God of Israel has entered by it." The east gate opens and looks toward the Mount of Olives and we know that when Jesus returns He will return to this mount. He will then enter Jerusalem by the east gate. The east gate then speaks of the return of Jesus Christ. But perhaps in a more now relevance to the Church is the scriptural truth that the Glory entered the Temple through the gate facing east. I believe as we allow the processes, and we have endured some of the restoration and rebuilding phases we will find that the pertinent application of the East Gate to our lives this moment in time- is the release of the Glory of God into the Temple.

Ezekiel 43:4 "The glory of the Lord entered the temple through the gate facing east."

The final gate to be rebuilt was called the Inspection Gate. It's kind of like anything that is being assembled or processed, before it I sent out or put on display it usually goes through an inspection process- checking out the soundness, stability and craftsmanship of what has been assembled. This gate is also known as the Miphkad gate. The word in Hebrew has a military connection and according to tradition it was at this gate that David would meet his troops to inspect them. This gate speaks to us of the examination of our lives by the Lord. This occurs-as indicated by Paul in 1 Cor 4:4: 'For I am conscious of nothing against myself, yet I am not by this acquitted; but the one who examines me is the Lord.'

Matthew 7: 15 "Beware of false prophets, which come to you in sheep's clothing, but inwardly they are ravening wolves.16 Ye, shall know them by their fruits. Do men gather grapes of thorns, or figs of thistles? 17 Even so every good tree bringeth forth good fruit; but a corrupt tree bringeth forth evil fruit. 18 A good tree cannot bring forth evil fruit, neither can a corrupt tree bring forth good fruit. 19 Every tree that bringeth not forth good fruit is hewn down, and cast into the fire.20 Wherefore, by their fruits ye shall know them".

In exploring all the gates that were in need of being restored in Jerusalem, in order for them to be a functioning community; I can see the relationship to us as individuals as well as communities. If we do not engage in these stages of development, and access these areas and their purposes to our lives, we may fail greatly when it comes time to go through the Inspection Gate.

13.
Completion

Harvest Time

Once the foundational work is done, and the walls and the gates are restored, then comes alignment for the assignment. Nehemiah 7:1-2 (NIV) "Now when the wall was rebuilt and I had set up the doors, and the gatekeepers and the singers and the Levites were appointed, then I put Hanani my brother, and Hananiah the commander of the fortress, in charge of Jerusalem, for he was a faithful man and feared God more than many."

There are two crucial aspects of those two verses. The first is after the structure was built, or rebuilt as this case was, then the singers, gatekeepers were positioned. Many are calling in the people they need to fill positions that are vacant in the Church, but it is not time for them. Not until in the spirit that position has been made ready, that aspect of the structure rebuilt that would pertain to them. The walls, gates, foundational work has not yet been done. Multitudes are in the balance awaiting their alignment for the assignment but their release to be positioned will not take place until the builders complete their part.

The second thing is Nehemiah was an Apostle, after completing this building project he turned it over to one that had been prepared by God to take over in his absence. Just because we build something or establish something does not mean it is ours. Apostles build, start a work, and a lot of times move on to the next project.

While the building project is being accomplished, there is as well mentoring, discipleship taking place. The Nehemiah of the group has to find his Hanani who is faithful, God fearing, and appointed by God to take over as Nehemiah goes forth to the next building project.

This as well promotes discipleship which is desperately needed. We are to be pouring out into people and preparing the younger generations even to take the baton and run the race when our time has come to shift into other areas. Crucial to know when it is our season to build, to preach, to oversee, to govern, to mentor. If we are operating in an area and functioning out of season we are hindering the flow of God.

Hindering the flow of God because of our out of season positioning stifles the way God intends to flow even through others. Nehemiah had to know his place, he knew when it was his season to lead in the rebuilding and once built he was no longer to be the leader in that capacity. For God had need of him in a new positioning. Hanani would never been given his chance to lead and fulfil what God had intended for him if Nehemiah had not allowed God to lead and move him on other directions as God willed.

After Nehemiah completed the rebuilding, he received yet another blueprint and set of instructions to begin to set order in the City. The structure was built, and now people were being positioned accordingly. Singers and Levites on the walls, gatekeepers at the gates, point guards in positions around the City.

The City having been rebuilt was spacious, and now it appeared that something was missing. This City that had been recently renovated needed people and houses to complete the establishing. Nehemiah 7: 5-6 (NAS) "Then my God put into my heart to assemble the nobles, the officials and the people to be enrolled by genealogies. Then I found the book of genealogy of those who came up first in which I found the following record: These are the people of the province who came up from the captivity of the exiles whom Nebuchadnezzar the king of Babylon had carried away, and who returned to Jerusalem and Judah, each to his city."

The previous scripture signifies that after the rebuilding, restoring, positioning and bringing order and alignment for the assignment; now it was time for the exiles, the prodigals, those scattered to return home. God in his infinite wisdom is not allowing the harvest to come to everyone right now. Some have to undergo some building processes. If not, nothing is really changed and the people that are as the scattered will return to find the same thing that they left.

When the Spirit of God begins to draw those who are not the builders, but the exiles or the prodigals we want them to see change and restoration. They want to be embraced by all things that have been made new. So that the issues that drove them away will not be there as well to welcome them.

We want the Church to be established and restored as was Jerusalem, readied for the exiles return. Everyone in their places, skilled in what their assignment is. Ready to meet the needs of the exiles, the prodigals when they come back. Those positioned on the walls and in the City equipped to mentor and disciple those that are drawn back, so that there is a Godly reproduction taking place.

Nehemiah was faithful with the assignment and the rebuilding project and Hanani was not the only one promoted, Nehemiah who once was a cupbearer for the king was now the Governor. He once served a king as a servant and now he was bestowed with a governmental mantle and kingly authority. He was faithful with little and now was ruler over much. Nehemiah did not begrudge his small beginnings, but allowed it to develop him inwardly as a leader.

Nehemiah 8:9-12 (NIV) "Then Nehemiah, who was the governor, and Ezra the priest and scribe, and the Levites who taught the people said to all the people, "This day is holy to the Lord your God; do not mourn or weep." For all the people were weeping when they heard the words of the law. Then he said to them, "Go, eat the fat, drink of the sweet, and send portions to him that has nothing prepared; for this day is Holy to the Lord. Do not be grieved, for the joy of the Lord is your strength." So the Levites calmed all the people, saying, "Be still, for the day is holy; do not be grieved." All the people went away to eat, to drink, to send portions and to celebrate a great festival, because they understood the words which had been made known to them."

Restoration, rebuilding, alignment and order- exiles back home; and now a celebration. The law was trying to steal the joy and the jubilance from the people that were so excited at what God had done for them. But Nehemiah proclaimed to them that it was good for them to experience joy, it was their strength. He spoke to the grief associated with law, and possibly even their past. For this rebuilding, and its completion was a sign of a new covenant.

This was not a day for grief, or weeping and being sorrowful. For God had done great things, and this was a new day. A day of a new covenant, and a new beginning. And it was HOLY TO THE LORD!

14.
Strategy from Nehemiah

Blueprint Revealed

This is some points of strategy that I have pulled out of the book of Nehemiah. I can see it as a proven Apostolic Strategy given to us as a blueprint to follow.

1. Receive the burden of the Lord. In a time of prayer and intercession it will begin to expand into an assignment or vision. Then the Spirit of God will begin to download into you the blueprint and strategy of how to go forth and accomplish it. If you only have a burden and not received the blueprint or strategy then you must spend more time in prayer. Birthing it out in the Spirit.
2. With the burden being birthed into a blueprint, then there will come an unlocking of favor. Which will connect you with the people that are called to work alongside of you as well as financially assist you. Provision for the vision.
3. Connect with and build relationships with those that God has called to this assignment. Discern who has been sent there to be as the army who will war with you as the building commences, as well as those who are joined with you as builders.
4. Do not disclose the plan, the dream, and assignment before time. Protect your seed. Be sure of those that you are disclosing it too. Make sure they are appointed to this assignment.
5. Nehemiah did his preparation at night, unseen by the masses. He spied the City at night while everyone was sleeping. So that no one could see his actions as he was preparing to implement strategy.
6. Know that even when opposition comes, the God of heaven will grant success.
7. Be sure the enemy has no place in the new thing, carried over from the former. If there was an assignment of the enemy against you or your Ministry and you are at a place of rebuilding, deal with it first. Take time in prayer to ensure that the issues that brought you to a place of devastation has been dealt with in the spirit and resolved. As I said do this before you begin the rebuilding project.

8. Resist the enemy, his temptations to entertain discouragement as well as his intimidations. Know that these are mere attempts to hinder you and the rebuilding if possible, or even stop your progression. Do not stop building no matter what the enemy says and or does.
9. Be sensitive to the condition of those who are assigned alongside of you. Discern their condition in the midst of warfare and rebuilding. Strengthen those that feel weak.
10. Unity must be a focus and an achievement. Especially between those called to the assignment at hand.
11. Use wisdom with the zeal that you have to see the Vision manifested and the assignment completed.
12. In all things remember God and give Him glory. For He is the author and the finisher of your faith, the assignment came from the Creator of heaven and earth. He entrusted you to bring forth into a place of manifestation a dimension of His Kingdom. So as you complete the work, and all are in positions fulfilling purpose. Rejoice and give Him Glory in every phase of rebuilding, no matter what the opposition.
13. Rebuild according to the guidance and blueprints of God.
14. Restore the foundations, pillars, walls, gates of the Ministry, Church or City first as a prelude to the harvest of souls.
15. Do not bow to the tactics of the enemy and compromise your spiritual positioning even if the enemy attempts to annihilate you with character assassination.
16. After the structure is established allow God to show you the positioning as well as positions needing to be filled. Also whom shall fill them? This is as well a part of the building process, setting order and bringing alignment. God flows through order not chaos.
17. In the midst of building keep a balance. There will be times of warfare in the midst of building.
18. Always be mentoring and training those around you. For those in your charge, God has purposed. It is up to us to be as Nehemiah and see the Hanani in someone.
19. Always speak quickly to any discouragement or any other enemy or weapon formed that is trying to prosper against you or the builders.
20. Maintain the joy of the Lord which is your strength. Guard it with all diligence.

15.
Working Of the Nehemiah Strategy

Take It to the Streets

1.   Prepare a people (teams) to go forth and possess the land. Engage in teaching and training that builds them up as individuals and equips them to go forth. Activating them.

2.   Develop prayer teams. I recommend 2 different types. You have some intercessors and warriors that have an anointing to pray for the Church, Leaders, and internal workings of the Church. First team can be called – "Repairers of Broken Walls". That is Team- Internal Warriors. They will concentrate on the rebuilding process within the 4 walls and then continue to cover as the move of God emerges. External Warriors- "Restorers of Streets with Dwellings"- are your die hard let me tear that devils head off intercessors. Those whose passion is spiritual warfare. They will concentrate on the warfare in the heavens, Principalities & Powers. They will as well pray over the territory and the building project in the Community.

3.   Gather together both prayer teams, as well as an evangelism team. Coordinate the Vision and Strategy, make a plan.

4.   Be sure that any needed rebuilding projects in regards to your Church or Ministry are completed. Make sure that you have a firm foundation, walls, gates, pillars in the Spirit are established and rebuilt in the Spirit. Prepared for the increase. The exiles shall return.

5.   Hold times of prayer. Even have times of City-Wide prayer connecting with other Ministries and Ministers in the land. Pastors, Ministry heads join in unity to cry out for your City.

6.   Begin to disciple the Community you are preparing to evangelize.

7.   Discipling- Organize times of training, community awareness, open the Church up for times of praying for the sick and their needs. Host Community events, cook outs etc.

8.   Begin to take teams and go door to door. Ask them if you can pray with them about anything. Most of the time, people will take a moment to let you pray for their needs. We have done this and found the response is usually great. Before you leave them, give them some contact info from your Church. Or an invite that has been prepared beforehand. Follow up with them if they say it is ok.

9. Take groups out into the community and establish walls of prayer surrounding the community you are planning to evangelize and disciple. Strategically place people where they are better suited, even in regards to street evangelism and community prayer. Establish team leaders who will be held accountable for sections of your territory in regards to evangelism and prayer. This will cause a more unified and yet concentrated effort giving them territory to govern and disciple within the territory. Plus this is as well a time of mentoring and discipleship for them. Developing leadership skills in them.

10. Be consistent in your contact throughout the Community. Let them see you restoring the walls, and dealing with any situations that attempt to overtake them, bring harm to or endanger the community you are charged to rule over.

11. Building relationships is a key to discipleship as well as evangelism; build trust.

12. If God has given you the City, success will come as you establish and build the wall one section at a time. Once you are successful in discipling and evangelizing- maintaining a section, expand your territory. Bringing restoration to a larger geographical area. Do not attempt to take the whole City at once. Even God told Joshua that he would drive out the "ITES" before him, a little at a time, one at a time. God knows you need to possess and maintain bit by bit. This is key to our effectiveness and progress. Only win, what you can maintain. Only set out to rebuild what you have builders for.

13. Remember Psalms 133, this must be a focus with every phase. Unity releases the Commanded blessing. Build relationships with community, Government leaders, other Churches and Ministries.

14. As a section of the wall is rebuilt, a victory is won, a phase is complete, and have a Celebration; just as Nehemiah did. Reinforcing the joy of harvest. Have times of praise & worship, establishing the Tabernacle of David in that land.

16.
Scriptures to Assist the Rebuilding Process

Roll Up Your Sleeves & Begin!

Speak to the demonically enforced walls, which stand as mountains of opposition around your soul.

1. "Let every mountain now hear the voice of the Lord and be removed- Micah 6:2
2. I command every mountain to be thou removed and cast into the sea- Mark 11:23
3. I declare that the mountain of Esau(works of the flesh) are laid to waste- Malachi 1:3
4. O God, You are opposition to every destroying mountain- Jeremiah 51:25
5. I declare these mountains melt like wax before the Lord- Psalms 97:5
6. No mountain of opposition shall stop me or prevent me from fulfilling destiny, for they shall be made as a plain before me-Zechariah 4:7

Speak to the assignment of the enemy against you.

1. The covenant with death is annulled, and any agreement with my enemy is broken.- Isaiah 28:18
2. I sever and break myself loose from all unholy covenants and agreements made between demonic forces and myself or my bloodline.- Exodus 23:32
3. I cancel all destruction concerning my gates.- Psalm 24:7

Speak to the Principalities & Powers

1. Let every false ministry in high place be removed.- 1 Kings 12:31

2. Let all false worship in high places be silenced and removed. 2 Chronicles 28:25
3. Let all religious spirits be cast down from their high places.- 2 Kings 23:8
4. Everywhere I walk, speak and declare over, let spirits of witchcraft be dealt with and overtaken. 2 Chronicles 28:4
5. Let us take authority over the Principalities and powers, evil in high places. 2 Chronicles 34: 3-7

Encourage & declare over yourself

1. You, O Lord, have given me the necks of my enemies; I will destroy them in Jesus Name.- Psalms 18:40
2. I will beat my enemies as fine as dust before the wind; I cast them out like dirt in the street.- Psalms 18:42
3. I overcome every unclean spirit because greater is He that is in me than he that is in the world.- 1 John 4:4
4. Teach my hands to war and my fingers to fight.- Psalms 144:1
5. I tread upon the head of the serpent and scorpion and over all the power of the enemy, and nothing by any means shall harm me.- Luke 10:19
6. Let every root of bitterness be uprooted over my life.- Hebrews 12:15

Speak to your walls

1. I declare there is a hedge of protection around my mind, body, soul & spirit. As well as around my possessions, loved ones, finances and family, in Jesus Name- Hosea 2:6
2. Bind up all breeches, O Lord- Isaiah 30:26
3. I declare every broken wall and hedge in my life that is meant to be erected and standing is repaired in Jesus Name.- Ecclesiastes 10:8
4. Let my walls be salvation and my gates praise.- Isaiah 60:18

Declare over your Nation
1. I pray my nation will bring forth the praises of God- Isaiah 60:6
2. I pray my nation will seek the Lord.- Isaiah 11:10

3. I pray that the Lord does a new thing in my nation. Isaiah 43:19-20
4. I pray that all children in my nation will be taught of the Lord.- Isaiah 54:13
5. I pray that my nation will be saved and walk in the light.- Revelation 21:24
6. I pray that all who walk in darkness in my nation will see the light that outshines the darkness.- Isaiah 9:2
7. Let your great wonders be done in my nation.-Psalms 96:3
8. Let the Kingdom of God manifest in my nation with righteousness, peace and joy in the Holy Spirit.- Romans 14:17
9. Let the Lord's dominion be established in my nation.- Psalm 72:8-9
10. Let every covenant with death and Hell be broken in my nation.- Isaiah 2:18
11. Let my nation be filled with the knowledge of the glory of the Lord, as the waters cover the seas.- Habakkuk 2:14
12. Lord, let all the idolaters in my nation be confounded and let them turn and worship you.- Psalm 97:7

Speak to the walls of your soul, City and Nation
1. I declare that just like the hand of God did concerning the walls of Jericho, so shall it be to every demonic wall around my life, City, or Nation.- Joshua 6:5
2. I declare that there is extensive work being done in the Spirit concerning the walls around my life, family, Ministry, City and Nation.- 2 Chronicles 27:3
3. I declare we are working hard to repair all the broken sections of the wall and even restoring the watchmen towers around them. These walls are double portioned and reinforced and are a support to the City of David.- 2 Chronicles 32:5
4. I declare the outer walls of the City & Nation are being rebuilt. 2 Chronicles 33:14
5. I declare that the wall of protection that God has given us restored every place it has been destroyed.- Ezra 9:9
6. I declare that all come and assist us in rebuilding the walls of Jerusalem.- Nehemiah 2:17
7. I declare that I am devoted to working on these walls.- Nehemiah 5:16

8.   I declare that the walls are rebuilt and standing tall as a protective hedge that keeps the enemy out of the borders of my life, City & Nation.- Jeremiah 39:2

9.   Let the walls of God surround us completely.- Ezekiel 40:5

10.   Let every wall be built true to plumb line.-Amos 7:7

11.   I declare you Lord are a wall of fire around my life, family, Ministry, City & Nation. And the glory of God is contained within.- Zechariah 2:5

12.   I declare that the walls of my City will be built on the foundation that you have laid. -Revelation 21:14

In Conclusion

I pray you have been inspired and illuminated by this teaching. Happy building! And I pray that God will do in you, for you and through you what only God can do….

Isaiah 61:4 (NIV) "They will rebuild the ancient ruins and restore the places long devastated; they will renew the ruined cities that have been devastated for generations."

Isaiah 58:12 (NIV) "Your people will rebuild the ancient ruins and will raise up the age old foundations; you will be called Repairer of Broken Walls, Restorer of Streets with Dwellings."

Isaiah 49:8-9 (NIV) "This is what the Lord says: "In the time of my favor I will answer you, and in the day of salvation I will help you; I will keep you and will make you to be a covenant for the people, to restore the land and to reassign its desolate inheritances, to say to the captives, 'Come out', and to those in darkness, 'Be free!' They will feed beside the roads and find pasture on every barren hill."

Isaiah 60:1 (NIV) "Arise, shine, for your light has come, and the glory of the Lord rises upon you."

Printed in Great Britain
by Amazon